HOW'S YOUR CLASSROOM?

A Guidebook on Navigating Action Research Process

Bernardo C. Lunar, PhD

A Guidebook on Navigating Action Research Process
By Bernardo C. Lunar

ISBN:
Hardbound-978-621-470-470-5
MOBI/KINDLE-978-621-470-471-2
Softbound/Paperback-978-621-470-472-9

Published by:
Poetry Planet Book Publishing House
Rosario, Pozorrubio, Pangasinan, Philippines
Contact Number: 09554960094
Email: maritesritumalta@gmail.com

ACKNOWLEDGMENT

The development and production of this guidebook were made possible by the contributions of the many people who supported me along the way:

First, my co-workers in the Graduate School and Office of Research, Evaluation and Publication. Working with these gifted professionals made each step of the process easier and more worthwhile;

Next, the teachers and students who served as respondents in the action researches that were featured in this book;

Also, to Poetry Planet Book Publishing team, for their diligent work in supporting my efforts to come up with a guidebook in action research that would be beneficial to both educators and students; and

Last, but most important of all, to my wife, Noemi, my son Josef Bernard, and my daughters Julia Angela, Joviene Ziela, and Jasmine Nimfa, for the inspiration.

Bernardo C. Lunar, PhD
Office of Research, Evaluation and Publication
San Pablo Colleges
Hermanos Belen St. San Pablo City
Laguna Province
bernardo.lunar@sanpablocolleges.edu.ph

(Please feel free to write or e-mail me with your comments, suggestions, and criticisms. I value your input and I hope that your comments will lead to a better revision of this guidebook in the future.)

FOREWORD

I have been asked as to where I draw my inspiration in accomplishing the Herculean jobs of being and staying as a researcher and as research manager– and the easiest way I can answer this is to draw on my own experience as a teacher. For me, being a researcher is something that has evolved from my innate passion to discover new knowledge. This responsibility is likewise unexpected, since it has not occurred to me that my hunger for knowledge may be something that I can concretely contribute to the research development of the institution. I have been able to reflect on the experiences I have acquired throughout the years I have spent in school as a researcher, research leader, and research manager, and these are the bases for the lessons that I have to offer in this guidebook.

From being a physical therapist, as a non- Education graduate, fate brought me to the teaching profession in 2002. Consequently, I became interested in the way in which the quality of teaching and learning experience I offer the students entrusted to me and the design and conduct of classes affect their behavior and their engagement. I effectively sensed the climate and quality of my relationship with the class and gradually learned to detect early warning signs and to find for ways of managing the classroom climate. My interest in research started with those little experiments in my own classroom. Thus, when

I wrote my thesis for the MEd Program (2008), I looked at the effect of the type of instruction on students' achievement in a more theorized way. It did not stop there. Soon after completing that paper, I utilized the findings of that research and worked on its recommendations. It gave rise to two more papers as I exhausted all possible studies from that single subject matter. That eventually led to the publication of my first book 'Human Anatomy and Physiology Study Partner (2009),' which is very much rooted to the kind of exploration that I initially employed as a new teacher in my class. Did I let it end there? After a term, that the book was used by my students, I designed a study to evaluate its effectiveness in attaining language and science skills. I believe these experiences collectively illustrate a simple answer to the question 'How did I become a researcher? It started with being curious and enquiring which certainly led me to become interested in the notion of reflective teaching.

Doing research is indeed a challenging job. As a full-time instructor in the college then, we were constantly expected to fulfill the triad functions of full-fledged educators: instruction, community involvement and research. In 2007, I received awards from my department for exemplary performance on instruction and community involvement. It challenged me to excel in research as well, thinking that I should be performing well in those three functions. Despite the demands of being a teacher, a program coordinator, a husband to my wife and a father to my children, I started doing research.

How do I get time to think - quality time, more specifically? With a teeming timetable already, how do I actually fit the responsibility of conducting research into my teaching profession? Cognizant that doing research is a tough job, I know I have to maintain a satisfactory quality of life. People say that a good researcher needs to maintain a valid grasp of reality. This is not possible by becoming a recluse. There were times when I had to hide away and communicate solely through my keyboard. I believe there is some responsibility to stay active and engaged in a normal way of life. Doing research necessitated me to negotiate, if not argue with the significant people in my life at home (my dear wife) and at work (my past and present superior) to try and find an approach to this drawback to research, so that they understand that hiding away and being far from them at times to research, study and present, is part of what I need to do and what I want to do. Aside from the thought of getting that research productivity award (which I got the following year), I believe there is a kind of noble intention which is underpinned by a moral concern in making a worthwhile contribution to the institution where I belong. For me, there are many personal costs involved in doing research; however, realizing that you are making dynamic contributions through your research endeavors seem to offset any disadvantage it brings.

How do I stay as a researcher? There are really a lot of tensions between and among job functions: teaching, administration, community extension and research. I employ one strategy I consider very effective in overcoming them. This is 'interfacing,' in which you look for research opportunities around the activities which you are required to engage in. Deeply motivated, I see my every professional and personal engagement an opportunity for conducting research. I was lucky to be given the opportunity to hold different posts in my area/ department and college. Most of my papers are geared towards addressing issues in the environment. This was because of the following reasons: 1) I was tasked to look after the environmental organization of students 2) I was chosen as one of the One Million Trees and Beyond champions of the school; 3) I was part of the Project Carbon Neutral Committee, 4) I used to be the head of the Center for the Environment; 5) I used to handle Environmental Science and Ecology Classes; and 6) I became part of the Steering Committee of the Tertiary Luzonian Ecocamp. I was able to write a few institutional researches because of being a program coordinator for the Certificate in Medical Transcription and being the Community Involvement Coordinator. With the various activities I spearhead and actively participate in, I can say that these are mine spot for lots of research problems waiting to be addressed by researchers.

On a final note, becoming a researcher must start from something you know and care for. You need to make the research process workable in your life – more specifically both in your work life and your personal life. You then work in a sustained way with your specialist focus and any support you can get from colleagues, friends and family.

Everyone must consider research as a worthwhile and rewarding thing to do. By this conviction, we can expect more members in the community who may be encouraged to actively engage in accomplishing researches and producing high quality work. This book will provide you with a practical guide on how to go about Action Research. May this guidebook mold you into a more pro-active and reflective teacher as you begin to ask yourself with the question- How is my classroom?

- BCL

TABLE OF CONTENTS

CHAPTER 1

Getting to Know What Action Research Is

We must find a way of bridging the traditional divide between Educational theory and professional practice. - Whitehead, J. (1988)

Action Research Described and Defined

Action research is a research that any of us can do on our own practice with the goal of improving it. It can be conducted with the assistance or guidance of professional researchers in order to improve strategies, practices, and knowledge of the environments within which they practice. Action research is a process in which participants examine their own educational practice, systematically and carefully, using the techniques of research.

Action Research is a method of conducting research that is collaborative, participatory, and empowering. It involves working with a group of people, such as a community or organization, to identify a problem or issue, collect and analyze data, and develop and implement solutions. The goal of action research is to improve practice and create positive change.

According to Mills (2000), educational action research is systematic inquiry done by teachers (or other individuals in an educational setting) to gather information about, and subsequently improve, the ways their particular educational setting operates, how they teach, and how well their students learn. Educational action research is used to solve an educational problem; help educators reflect on their own experiences; to address school-wide problems; and when teachers desire to improve their teaching pro-active.

Why is there a need to conduct educational action research? This type of action research gives educators new opportunities to reflect on and assess their teaching; explore and test new ideas, methods, and materials; assess how effective the new approaches are; share feedback with fellow team members; and make decisions about which new approaches to include in the practice.

History of Action Research Traced

The history of action research can be traced back to the early 20th century, with the work of Kurt Lewin, who is often considered the "father of action research." Lewin believed that research should be closely tied to practice and that the goal of research should be to improve the lives of people. He developed a three-step process for action research, known as the "Lewinian Cycle" which included: planning, acting, and evaluating.

In the 1950s, a group of educators in the United States began to adapt Lewin's ideas to the field of education. They emphasized the importance of involving practitioners in the research process and the use of action research to improve educational practice. The work of these educators, including Ralph Tyler, Paul L. Dressel, and Eugene E. Harris, was instrumental in establishing action research as a legitimate approach to educational research.

In the 1960s and 1970s, the field of action research expanded to include researchers in other fields, such as health care, organization development, and community development. The ideas of Lewin and the educational action researchers were further developed and expanded upon by researchers such as Peter Reason, John Heron, and David Coghlan.

In recent years, there has been a growing emphasis on participatory and collaborative forms of action research, such as participatory action research (PAR) and collaborative action research (CAR). These approaches involve working closely with community members and other stakeholders to identify problems, collect and analyze data, and develop and implement solutions.

Key Philosophies Related to Action Research Identified

There are several key philosophies that underlie action research. These are collaboration, empowerment, reflectivity; and praxis.

Collaboration: Action research is a collaborative process that involves working with a group of people to identify problems, collect and analyze data, and develop and implement solutions.

Empowerment: Action research is empowering in that it allows people to take control of their own lives and work towards positive change.

Reflectivity: Action research is reflective in that it encourages people to think critically about their practice and to make changes based on what they have learned.

Praxis: Action research is praxis-oriented in that it aims to bridge the gap between theory and practice, and to improve practice through the application of research.

Key Characteristics of Academic Action Research Pointed Out

Educational action research has been popular since it has a practical focus. It centers on a particular problem that will have immediate benefits to a single teacher, a group of teachers, school and communities. It is a self-reflective research process as educator-researchers turn their lenses on their own educational practices. It is collaborative as it may necessitate formation of a collaborative team from among the teachers, staff, students, community stakeholders, parents and administrators. It is also seen as a dynamic process of spiraling back and forth among reflection, data collection, and action. It does not follow a linear patter, neither does it follow a causal sequence from problem to action. Once data have been collected, analyzed and interpreted, findings shall be used as a basis decision making relative to Covid-19 pandemic.

From the findings of the study, the action researcher then develops a plan of action, be it forma or informal. Action researchers are not specifically interested in publication but is more concerned in sharing with individuals or groups. Stakeholders need to know the findings of our survey as soon as passable.

Educational action research may either be practical action research or participatory action research. Practical action research looks into local practices involving an individual or team- based inquiry. It focuses on teacher development and student learning. It involves implementation of a plan of action. Employing this design makes the teacher take the stance of a researcher. On the other hand, in participatory action research, local issues that constrain individual lives are studied. It emphasizes equal collaboration among participants all focusing on life-enhancing changes. Employing this design results to being an emancipated research.

CHAPTER 2

Sailing Across the Action Research Process

The journey of a thousand miles begins with one step.- Lao Tzu

The action research process typically involves several steps, which may vary depending on the specific approach being used. The following is a general overview of the steps that are commonly involved in the action research process:

Problem identification: The first step in the action research process is to identify a problem or issue that is of concern to the community or organization. This is the most crucial part of the process as it is believed that a perfect solution to a problem only begins when the real problem is identified. This may involve conducting a literature review, surveying community members, or holding focus groups to gather information about the problem.

Planning: Once a problem has been identified, the next step is to plan the research. This may involve developing a research question, determining the data that will be collected, identifying the research design and identifying the methods that will be used to collect and analyze the data.

Data collection: This step involves gathering data to answer the research question. Data collection methods may include surveys, interviews, observations, and document analysis. Data collection techniques may be in the form of 3 E's: Experiencing, Enquiring, Examining.

Data analysis: This step involves analyzing the data that has been collected. Depending on the research design, be it quantitative, qualitative, or a mixed- method design, this may involve coding and categorizing the data, identifying patterns and themes, and interpreting the results.

Intervention and evaluation: After the data have been analyzed, the next step is to develop and implement solutions or interventions to address the problem that was identified. This may involve working with the community or organization to develop a plan of action. As the intervention is implemented, the researcher should evaluate its effectiveness and make any necessary adjustments.

Dissemination and reflection: The final step in the action research process is to share the results of the research with the community or organization and reflect on what was learned. This may involve writing a report, presenting the findings at a conference, or holding a community meeting to share the results.

Take note that each step of the process can be a point of entry for action research. This means that one may start with the evaluation phase should there be an existing intervention already. If data sets are already available, such data can be analyzed to come up with an appropriate intervention.

It is likewise important to have in mind that action research is an iterative process, meaning that the steps may be repeated multiple times throughout the course of the research.

CHAPTER 3

Choosing the Right Approach to Action Research

Success is simple. Do what's right, the right way, at the right time.- Arnold H. Glasow

There are several different approaches to action research, each with its own unique perspective and focus. Some of the most common approaches include:

Critical action research: Critical action research is an approach that focuses on addressing issues of social inequality and injustice. This approach is often used to examine power imbalances and to empower marginalized communities. Critical action researchers aim to uncover the underlying structural and systemic factors that contribute to social problems and to work with communities to develop strategies for addressing these issues.

Feminist action research: Feminist action research is an approach that is informed by feminist theory and is concerned with addressing issues of gender inequality and oppression. This approach often involves working with women and other marginalized groups to identify the ways in which gender shapes their experiences and to develop strategies for addressing these issues.

Participatory action research (PAR): Participatory action research (PAR) is an approach that emphasizes the participation of community members and other stakeholders in the research process. PAR is often used to examine issues that are important to the community and to develop solutions that are relevant and meaningful to them. This approach also enables community members to take an active role in the research process, providing them with the skills and knowledge to continue working towards positive change long after the research has ended.

Collaborative action research (CAR): Collaborative action research (CAR) is an approach that emphasizes collaboration between researchers, practitioners and community members. This approach is used to address practical issues and improve the work of organizations. CAR is often used in professional fields such as education, health care, and social work to improve practice by working with community members and other stakeholders to identify problems, collect and analyze data, and develop and implement solutions.

Action science: Action science is an approach that emphasizes the understanding of organizational processes as well as the use of research as a means for organizational change. The research process is used to identify problems, design solutions and implement changes to improve the organization's performance.

Each of these approaches has its own strengths and limitations and it is important to choose the approach that best fits the research question and the context of the study. It's also important to note that some researchers may use a combination of approaches, tailoring their approach to the specific context and research question.

CHAPTER 4

Employing Different Strategies in Conducting Action Research

Strategy is not the consequence of planning, but the opposite: its starting point.- Henry Mintzberg

There are several strategies that can be used when working with communities and organizations to conduct action research. Some of these strategies include:

Building relationships: Building strong relationships with community members and organizational stakeholders is crucial for successful action research. This may involve spending time in the community or organization to get to know the people and their concerns, developing trust, and listening actively to their perspectives.

Empowering community members and organizational stakeholders: Action research is an empowering process that allows community members and organizational stakeholders to take an active role in the research process. This may involve providing training and support to help them collect and analyze data, as well as encouraging them to take an active role in developing and implementing solutions.

Building a shared understanding: Creating a shared understanding of the problem and the research process is important for successful action research. This may involve holding meetings or workshops to discuss the problem and the research process, and encouraging open and honest communication throughout the research process.

Being flexible: Flexibility is important when working with communities and organizations to conduct action research. This may involve being open to changing the research question or methods as needed, and being willing to make adjustments to the research process based on the needs and perspectives of the community or organization.

Being transparent and participatory: Action research is a transparent process that involves involving community members and organizational stakeholders in the research process. This may involve providing regular updates on the progress of the research, involving community members and organizational stakeholders in the data collection and analysis process, and sharing the results of the research with the community or organization.

Providing feedback and support: Providing feedback and support to community members and organizational stakeholders throughout the research process is important for successful action research. This may involve providing regular check-ins to discuss the progress of the research, providing support and guidance as needed, and working closely with community members and organizational stakeholders to develop and implement solutions.

It is important to note that the specific strategies used will depend on the context of the research and the needs of the community or organization. It is likewise important to be aware of the power dynamics that may exist and to take steps to address any imbalances of power.

CHAPTER 5

Addressing Issues when Conducting Action Research

Writing the perfect paper is a lot like a military operation. It takes discipline, foresight, research, strategy, and, if done right, ends in total victory.- Ryan Holiday

Issues to consider when conducting action research, such as power dynamics and ethical considerations. When conducting action research, there are several important issues to consider, including power dynamics and ethical considerations. Some of the specific issues that researchers may encounter include:

Power dynamics: Action research is often used to address issues of social inequality and injustice, and power imbalances may exist between the researcher and the community or organization being studied. It's important for researchers to be aware of these power dynamics and to take steps to address them. This may involve involving community members and organizational stakeholders in the research process, being transparent about the research process and findings, and working to build trust and relationships with the community or organization.

Ethical considerations: Action research raises a number of ethical considerations, such as the potential for exploitation, the protection of participant's rights, and the confidentiality of data. It's important for researchers to obtain informed consent from participants, to protect their rights and to respect their confidentiality. Researchers should also be mindful of the potential for exploitation, and should take steps to minimize any harm that may be caused as a result of the research.

Role of researcher: In action research, the researcher is also a participant, not only an observer. The researcher should be aware of the potential conflicts of interest that may arise and should take steps to minimize them. This may involve involving community members and organizational stakeholders in the research process, being transparent about the research process and findings, and working to build trust and relationships with the community or organization.

Potential for bias: Action research is often used to address issues of social inequality and injustice, and bias may exist in the data collection and analysis process. It's important for researchers to be aware of the potential for bias, to take steps to minimize it and to report any bias in the research findings.

Sustainability and scalability: Action research is often used to address practical problems, however it is important to consider the potential impact of the research and its ability to be sustained and scaled up.

By being aware of these issues and taking steps to address them, researchers can ensure that their action research is conducted in an ethical and responsible manner.

There are several strategies that can be used when working with communities and organizations to conduct action research.

CHAPTER 6

Zeroing into Classroom Action Research

"There's a way to do it better. Find it." – Thomas Edison

Classroom action research is a specific type of action research that is conducted by teachers in their own classrooms. This approach is often used to improve teaching practice and student learning. Classroom action research typically involves the same steps discussed on the previous chapter, which include:

Problem identification: The first step in classroom action research is for the teacher to identify a problem or issue that is of concern in their classroom. This may be related to student learning, behavior, or other classroom-related issues and programs.

Planning: Once a problem has been identified, the teacher will develop a plan for how to address it. This may involve identifying the research question, determining the data that will be collected, and identifying the methods that will be used to collect and analyze the data.

Data collection: This step involves gathering data to answer the research question. Data collection methods may include observations, student assessments, interviews, and surveys.

Data analysis: This step involves analyzing the data that has been collected. This may involve coding and categorizing the data, identifying patterns and themes, and interpreting the results.

Intervention and evaluation: After the data have been analyzed, the teacher will develop and implement strategies or interventions to address the problem that was identified. This may involve making changes to their teaching practice, providing additional support to students, or modifying the classroom environment. As the intervention is implemented, the teacher will evaluate its effectiveness and make any necessary adjustments.

Dissemination and reflection: The final step in the classroom action research process is to share the results of the research with other teachers and to reflect on what was learned. This may involve writing a report, presenting the findings at a conference, or holding a meeting with other teachers to share the results.

Owing to its nature as an action research, classroom action research is an iterative process, meaning that the steps may be repeated multiple times throughout the course of the research. This approach allows teachers to continuously improve their practice and adapt to the specific needs of their students.

Classroom action research has several advantages, it allows teachers to explore the specific needs of their students and to implement changes that are tailored to their classroom context. It also enables teachers to take an active role in their own professional development, and to reflect on and improve their practice. Additionally, it provides teachers with the opportunity to share their findings with other educators and contribute to the wider educational community.

CHAPTER 7

Appreciating Classroom Action Research Through Samples

If you're going to talk the talk, you've got to walk the walk".- Unknown

There are three data collection techniques that could be used for action research: through experiencing, through enquiring, or through examining. The sample action research papers here are grouped according to how the research data were collected.

A. THROUGH EXPERIENCING

This collection technique is done by observing how things are going. One can either be a passive or an active observer. In the example below, the researchers were passive observers.

Sample 1.

Implementation Of Transformative Learning Design In Environmental Science: An Action Research

Published in : *Global Research Journal on Mathematics and Science Education Vol. 2 No. 1 May 2013*

*Bernardo Lunar, Dr. Irish Dimaculangan,Marisol Laguardia,
Catherine Precioso, Dr. Joy Talens

Abstract

This action research was aimed at determining the internal strengths and weaknesses and external opportunities and threats in the implementation of transformative learning design in the Environmental Science course of De La Salle Lipa, Lipa City. Using the descriptive method of research, this study specifically used the SWOT Analysis in its approach to assessment of the major variables concerned.

Results of the study revealed that the following are the strengths of transformative learning: achievement of the three Lasallian attributes (ELGAs) such as critical thinker, excellent communicator and social responsible citizen through holistic approach; final product/performance task which is the first "Environmental Concert for A Cause" became the basis of learning; and, teachers became creative, imaginative and experimental in design and implementation. In terms of weaknesses, the following were identified; time constraints for planning and practicing for the concert; size of the class; and, the rubrics or basis for grading the students were not uniform for all teachers. The following were the opportunities identified: linking and networking with public and private sectors; more interesting teaching – learning strategies considering multiple intelligences and individual differences; and, profound information and research targets. The identified threats were: security and safety of students and teachers during field/outdoor activities and concert due to lack of adult or teacher companions; collection of regulation was inadequate; and resistance of parents and guardians in allowing students to participate in various activities.

In consideration of the findings of this study, an action plan has been developed to serve as a tool and guide to management and supervision of the implementation of transformative learning to continuously improve teaching and learning. This study recommends among all others the need to enhance the implementation of transformative learning in the course Environmental Science and the utilization of the action plan developed for such a purpose. Furthermore, a yearly assessment of the said program, a replication of this study perhaps, in another Science subjects, a conduct of comparative study of transformative learning between and among different subjects and further validation of the proposed plan, may also be taken into consideration in future teaching and learning endeavours.

Key words: transformative learning, environmental science, SWOT analysis

However, in the sample presented below, the researcher assumed an active stance during the observation.

Sample 2. Assessment of the Delivery of Distance Education with Asynchronous Learning (DEAL) of the AHEAD Learning Platform of San Pablo Colleges' Graduate School

Published in: San Pablo Colleges Research Journal Volume 10, February 2023

*Bernardo C. Lunar and **Eisen A. Perez

Abstract

During the pandemic, the instructional strategy employed in the Graduate School Department of San Pablo Colleges is Distance Education with Asynchronous Learning (DEAL). In this study, a total 137 graduate fellows enrolled in Master of Arts in Education, Master of Arts in Nursing and Doctor of Education assessed the level of their satisfaction and perceived effectiveness and relative advantage of DEAL compared to traditional in-school instructional mode. Results showed graduate fellows have very high level of satisfaction regarding the delivery of the teaching-learning process under the DEAL strategy. Majority of the areas under the delivery of the educative process were regarded as very highly satisfying including the use of technology, instructional medium, learning content, group discussions, and feedback mechanisms. fellows have high level of satisfaction as regards the provision of learning support under the DEAL strategy. Further, graduate fellow respondents consider DEAL as very highly effective as it works well with their work schedule and very highly advantageous as its more economical and practically recommendable compared to the traditional in-school instruction before the pandemic. Such findings justify the continuation of the current delivery mode of instruction for the succeeding semesters in the graduate school.

Keywords: graduate school, distance education, asynchronous learning, learning continuity

Introduction

During the time of pandemic and even in the new normal, NO LEARNER SHOULD BE LEFT BEHIND. Cognizant of the fact that not all learners are tailored for online learning, careful planning on how to go about the delivery of instruction should be made. Along this light, SPC thought about blended options, navigated flexible learning opportunities, reformulated the triad concerning learning objective-instruction-assessment, and embraced the **A**lternative **H**ybrid **E**ducation and **A**synchronous **D**istance Learning (**AHEAD Learning**) as San Pablo College's distinctive Instructional Model in accordance to government restrictions on holding of classes (Lunar et.al, 2022).

The following strategies shall be employed with variations in objectives, delivery of instruction, and assessment based on capability of learners to do self-care and their readiness for online and distance learning: 1. **H**ome-based **E**ducation **L**earning **M**ode **(HELM)** for Grade School; **H**ybrid **E**ducation **L**earning **P**rogram **(HELP)** for High School and College and **D**istance **E**ducation with **A**synchronous **L**earning **(DEAL)** for Graduate School (Saldua, 2022).

DEAL refers to the education style for self-motivated graduate school students who can deal with their work whenever they please either by modular class, online class or its combination. Using an LMS as tool of instruction, integrative approach to learning shall be practiced. Examinations shall be remotely administered and taken using the LMS platform. Students may report to school for defense, revalida and required seminars, fora and the likes.

In order to ascertain the directions to go after a year of implementing the DEAL, an assessment of its delivery was deemed necessary. The study sought to assess the fellows' level of satisfaction relative to the delivery of the teaching-learning process and provision of support service as the distinctive strategy for the graduate school is actualized. Likewise, it ascertained the perceived effectiveness and relative advantage of the DEAL compared to traditional mode of delivery pre-pandemic, aimed at developing an action plan that targets to enhance such delivery mode.

Methods

The study employed a descriptive research design. The descriptive method is a fact-finding procedure that includes analysis and interpretation of data. It is useful to describe answers to questions of who, what, where, and how (Burns, Alvin & Bush, 2009). It was adopted because the researchers believe it is fit to assess the fellows perception and assessment of the delivery mode,. The survey was the method used to gather the quantitative data needed. Using opportunity sampling, the study involved a total of 137 graduate fellows of SPC. Data gathering was made in the last two weeks of March 2021. The confidentiality of the responses that were gathered from them was guaranteed. A researcher-made questionnaire used was adopted used in the form of. Google form. The confidentiality of the responses that were gathered from them was guaranteed. From The data derived from the respondents' answers were then carefully recorded, tallied, tabulated statistically, analysed, and then interpreted.

Results and Discussion

Based on the online survey results, Table 1 presents the level of satisfaction of the graduate fellows with the DEAL in terms of the delivery of teaching- learning process and on the provision of learning support during the educative process.

The composite mean value of 4.01, verbally interpreted as very high, connotes that the graduate fellows have very high level of satisfaction regarding the delivery of the teaching-learning process under the DEAL strategy. Majority of the areas under the delivery of the educative process were regarded as very highly satisfying including the use of technology, instructional medium, learning content, group discussions, and feedback mechanisms. As regards the assessment of learning materials and session facilitation showed that fellows were highly satisfied.

Table 1. Level of Satisfaction with DEAL

On Delivery of Teaching-Learning Process	Mean	VI
Instructional Medium	4.04	Very high
Learning Content	4.03	Very high
Learning Materials	3.83	High
Group Discussions	4.02	Very high
Use of technology	4.08	Very high
Feedback mechanisms	4.01	Very high
Session facilitation	4.00	High
Composite Mean	**4.01**	**Very High**
On Provision of Learning Support	**Mean**	**VD**
Work Load Considerations	4.02	Very high
Disseminating Pertinent Information	3.95	High
Feedback on Program of Study	3.91	High
Learning facilities and Resources	3.92	High
Student Curricular and Co-Curricular Activities	4.02	Very high
Composite Mean	**3.94**	**High**

The very high satisfaction level of the graduate fellows can be attributed to the maximization of the functionalities of the proprietary Learning Management System (LMS) that SPC subscribes to that is Brightspace (BS). With BS, Immediate feedbacks were given and a platform was provided for discussion forum for the fellows. Information sharing was easy with as learning materials are securely kept as LMS contents. As mentioned by Alturki and

Aldraiweesh (2021) using LMS during the pandemic would enhance efficiency. Perceived utility is a crucial determinant of purpose to embrace more creative and user-friendly innovations that allow them greater flexibility. The findings of the current study also support that of Vord and Pogue's (2012) that suggests that while face to face instruction requires more time per student, certain aspects of online teaching take considerably more time per student than in a face to face classroom.

Teachers do value tools within the learning management system and overall feel value from its interaction. They especially value the ability to transmit documents and efficient communication enabled through the system. Iqbal and Qureshi (2011) suggest the following factors as the most important considerations when selecting a learning management system: organizational goals and objectives, technical specification and support, design specifications, clear and user friendly graphical interface, well designed course repository, course administration capability, capability of interaction among users, evaluation and feedback, student's profile, and pedagogy.

On the other hand, with the composite mean value of 3.94, verbally interpreted as high connotes that the fellows have high level of satisfaction as regards the provision of learning support under the DEAL strategy. Only two areas assessed were regarded by the fellows with very high satisfaction level, these are workload considerations and students' activities. Majority of the areas assessed were regarded as highly satisfying including the dissemination of pertinent school information, feedback on program of study and on learning facilities and resources.

Such findings can be explained by the advantage of asynchronous distance learning as this favors the varying work situations and demands of the fellows. Various online capacity building, enhancement webinars, and formation activities were also provided to the fellows despite the physical distance brought about by mobility restrictions during the pandemic. Leaders in student affairs and services see their roles as complements to the academic function whereby the support they offer to students lays the foundation for student success in higher education and beyond as students graduate and begin to contribute to society at-large (Ludeman & Schreider, 2020). Importantly, student support services foster a sense of belonging for the students (Pelletier, 2020).

Prior to the pandemic, most student support services were provided on-campus and since student support personnel tended to have less physical contact with online students, they may not have fully appreciated that particular population's expectations and perceptions (Forrester & Parkinson, 2006). Literature confirms that most institutions are not providing equitable student support services to online students, with the most significant gaps identified in student advising and counseling services (Barr, 2014; Brown, 2017; Cooper, Gin & Brownell, 2019; Currie,

2010; Forrester & Parkinson, 2006; Hicks, 2016). It is surprising to note that the graduate fellows have high regards on the students support provided to them.

As institutions and students face longer-term needs for remote teaching and learning, experts caution that students may need more support than ever as they face new stressors around their mental, social, and financial health (Blankstein et al., 2020; Burke, 2020; Hinton, 2020). Students were and are also experiencing life disruptions such as becoming ill, job loss, taking care of a sick family member, or home-schooling children (Blankstein et al., 2020; Educationdata.org, n.d.; Fishman & Hiler, 2020; Garrett et al., 2020). In fact, students may find it even more difficult to stay motivated in their learning, presently, as they balance working obligations and family needs (Blankstein et al., 2020; Fishman & Hiler, 2020; Hinton, 2020), suggesting a heightened need for scaffolding student support that can be offered virtually.

Table 2 below presents the perceived effectiveness and relative advantage of DEAL over the traditional in-school instruction before the pandemic. As gleaned on the table, graduate fellow respondents consider DEAL as very highly effective (x=4.04) as it works well with their work schedule and very highly advantageous as it is more economical (x=4.03) and practically recommendable (x=4.01) compared to the traditional in-school instruction before the pandemic. Moreover, the fellows also consider the DEAL as more convenient, comfortable and effective than the traditional mode of delivery of instruction. They further claim that DEAL is more preferred than face-to-face sessions as it allows more student engagement and better learning opportunity.

Table 2. Perceived Effectiveness and Relative Advantage of DEAL

Perceived Effectiveness and Relative Advantage	Mean	VI	Rank
More effective than traditional	3.96	high	5
Better learning opportunity	3.79	high	8
More preferred than traditional	3.83	high	6
Allows more student engagement	3.85	high	7
Works well with work schedule	4.04	Very high	1
More convenient and comfortable	3.99	high	4
More economical	4.03	Very high	2
Practically recommendable	4.01	Very high	3

This is supported by the claim in literature that when the students' satisfaction levels are analyzed in the study of Gonçalves et al., 2020; Avsheniuk et al., 2021; Bakhov et al., 2021; Glebov et al., 2021; Todri et al., 2021) that the students' satisfaction levels are high. When students compare face-to-face and online learning methods, they state that online learning has opportunities to compensate for their deficiencies due to the pandemic conditions (Abrosimova, 2020). Though there are counter claims as well pointing out to moderate and low students' satisfaction with distance education and asynchronous learning (Viktoria and Aida, 2020; Aldossary, 2021; Didenko et al., 2021 Taşkaya, 2021).

In the same manner, when students compare face-to-face and online learning methods, they state that online learning has opportunities to compensate for their deficiencies due to the pandemic conditions (Abrosimova, 2020). Contrastingly. for other students, they prefer face-to-face learning (Gonçalves et al., 2020; Kaisar and Chowdhury, 2020; Bakhov et al., 2021). Students' positive attitudes and levels of satisfaction with their distant education programs have an impact on their ability to profit from the program. Consequently, schools wishing to implement distant education should begin by developing a structure, content, and pedagogical approach that would improve the satisfaction of their students. There is no universally applicable magic formula since student satisfaction differs depending on the country, course content, and external factors (Masalimova et.al 2022).

Conclusions and Recommendations

Based on the foregoing findings, it can be concluded that graduate fellows are highly satisfied with the

DEAL as strategic instructional delivery in the graduate school. They consider the DEAL as highly effective. DEAL is regarded as very highly advantageous as it works well with their work schedule; more economical, and practically recommendable compared to the traditional in-school instruction before the pandemic. In the light of the conclusions drawn, future directions were ascertained as regards the continuation of the employment of DEAL as instructional mode of delivery in the graduate school. Further refinement and enhancement in areas found to have relatively lower acceptability by the respondents were addressed in the action plan that was put forward as an output of this study

References

- Abrosimova, G. A. (2020). Digital literacy and digital skills in university study. Int. J. High. Educ. 9, 52–58. doi: 10.5430/ijhe.v9n8p52
- Aldossary, K. (2021). Online distance learning for translation subjects: tertiary level instructors' and students' perceptions in Saudi Arabia. Turk. Online J. Distance Educ. 22:6.
- Bakhov, I., Opolska, N., Bogus, M., Anishchenko, V., and Biryukova, Y. (2021). Emergency distance education in the conditions of COVID-19 pandemic: experience of Ukrainian universities. Educ. Sci. 11:364. doi: 10.3390/educsci11070364
- Didenko, I., Filatova, O., and Anisimova, L. (2021). COVID-19 lockdown challenges or new

era for higher education. Propós. Represent. 9:e914. doi: 10.20511/pyr2021.v9nspe1.914

- Glebov, V. A., Popov, S. I., Lagusev, Y. M., Krivova, A. L., and Sadekova, S. R. (2021). Distance learning in the humanitarian field amid the coronavirus pandemic: risks of creating barriers and innovative benefits. Propós. Represent. 9:e1258. doi: 10.20511/pyr2021.v9nspe3.1258

- Gonçalves, S. P., Sousa, M. J., and Pereira, F. S. (2020). Distance l

- earning perceptions from higher education students—the case of Portugal. Educ. Sci. 10:374. doi: 10.3390/educsci10120374

- Kaisar, M. T., and Chowdhury, S. Y. (2020). Foreign language virtual class room: anxiety creator or healer? Engl. Lang. Teach. 13:130. doi: 10.5539/elt.v13n11p130

- Lunar, B. (2020). Blueprint of the Conduct of School Year 2020-2021: AHeAD Learning Platform of San Pablo Colleges. Maestra Journal

- Saldua, M.R. (2022). Internal Strategic Analysis of Home Education Learning Mode (HELM) of San Pablo Colleges: Cornerstone for an Enhancement Plan. Unpublished Master's Thesis

- Taşkaya, S. M. (2021). Teacher candidates' evaluation of the emergency remote teaching practices in turkey during COVID-19 pandemic. Int. J. Progress. Educ. 17, 63–78. doi: 10.29329/ijpe.2021.366.5

- Todri, A., Papajorgji, P., Moskowitz, H., and Scalera, F. (2021). Perceptions regarding distance learning in higher education, smoothing the transition. Contemp. Educ. Technol. 13:e287. doi: 10.30935/cedtech/9274

Sample 3.

Research Themes and Desired Capabilities of a Higher Educational Institution in Line with Integrated Coastal Management: An Action Research

*Bernardo C. Lunar, Catherine M. Precioso, Jesirene R. Villanueva, Richard M. Magsino

Presented at International Conference in Social Sciences, Health and Environment 2013, September 24-26, 2013, Sydney Harbour Marriott Hotel, Sydney, Australia

Abstract

Integrated Coastal Management (ICM) is a mechanism that involves a systematic process for managing the competing issues in marine and coastal areas, including diverse and multiple uses of natural resources. De La Salle Lipa (DLSL), as an ICM Training Center and an active partner of

Conservation International-Philippines in the Coral Triangle Initiative, envisions the establishment of a functional Lasallian Center for the Environment which shall serve as think-tank for the implementation of the projects pertaining to ICM. This action research identified the desired capacities along the identified environmental research themes: Integrated Coastal Management and Integrated Information Management System; Biodiversity, Resource Management and Pollution Control; and Mangrove Reforestation and Monitoring Program. It also assessed the internal strengths and weaknesses and external opportunities and threats of the institution as regards coastal resource management research. Research capacity gaps were then extracted from the weaknesses and threats identified. These include the need for avenues for hands-on ICM related works and information management trainings; need for specific skills on resource management, pollution control and biodiversity studies; and the need for capacity enhancement as regards mangrove reforestation and monitoring. An action plan for each research theme was drafted as an output of this study.

Keywords: Marine Science, research themes, Integrated Coastal Management, action plan, De La Salle Lipa, Philippines.

Introduction

Anchored in the Environmental Policy of the institution, De La Salle Lipa is commited to exercise, by all means, practicable and through all available resources, stewardship of the environment in which it is a part of. In the pursuit of its vision-mission and strategic objectives, it ensures that the campus is safe, secure, healthy, environmentally friendly and conducive for working and learning. It is for this purpose that DLSL has forged partnership and collaboration with Conservation International- Philippines (CI-P) and Partnerships in Environmental Management for the Seas of East Asia (PEMSEA).

On one hand, PEMSEA is a regional partnership programme implemented by the United Nations Development Programme and executed by the United Nations Office for Project Services. PEMSEA's areas of work include coastal and ocean governance, natural and man-made hazard prevention and management, habitat protection, restoration and management, water use and supply management, pollution and waste reduction management, as well as food security and livelihood management. One of the important tasks that PEMSEA assumes is turning the knowledge about regional coastal into action that can improve the status quo. PEMSEA capitalizes on its broad intergovernmental, financial and intellectual resources to come up with the best solutions problems of sustainable coastal management (PEMSEA.org, 2013).

On the other hand, CI is a valued partner and trusted advisor in biodiversity conservation, helping to provide the scientific basis to guide protected area designation decisions and serving as member to several protected area management boards, working with the national government and other partners. In order to address urgent threats to the Philippines' biodiversity, CI is pursuing a strategy that values and protects healthy ecosystems and its services to the Filipino people and to the rest of the world. CI in the Philippines focuses on thematic responses supported by field demonstration in priority areas (Conservation International Philippines, 2013).

As an active partner in the different programs of not only the CI-P and PEMSEA, but also the provincial and local governments in Batangas, DLSL takes part in the related projects including but not limited to the Coral Triangle Initiative, Verde Island Passage Marine Corridor, Calumpang River Rehabilititation and University Mentoring Program. It is also designated as the ICM Learning Center in Luzon having trained some of its faculty members as ICM trainers. As envisioned, a functional Center for the Environment (CFE) shall serve as repository and think-tank for the research and development projects on resource management and environmental protection and conservation. It is for this reason that this descriptive study was conducted aimed at identifying the institution's research themes from which desired learning capabilities and research capacity gaps were drawn. Findings will serve as basis for future directions to be taken by DLSL in the areas of research and extension pertaining to coastal resource management.

Methods

The descriptive method of research was used in the study specifically employing SWOT Analysis in its approach to assessment of the major variables concerned. It is undertaken to understand the internal and external environments of a certain process or firm. Upon careful analysis of the environmental situation or conduct of a process or project, assessors come to know the strengths and weaknesses and identify the opportunities provided and threats posed by the environment. It is a systematic approach to formulate strategic policies and corrective steps for improvement. After conducting SWOT Analysis, action planning should follow. The action plan specifies the actions needed to address each of the organizational issues and to reach each of the associated goals (McNamara, 2011).

This action research involved five faculty members from the Biology Department and Science Area under the College of Education, Arts and Sciences. These faculty members are actively involved in the projects of CI and PEMSEA as regards coastal resource management. Data and other information needed in this study were gathered mainly through open–ended questionnaire, unstructured interview, and documentary analysis.

Results and Discussion

In consonance with the anchored on the research priority area of the institution as regards Health, Environment, Safety and Security, it is envisioned that a functional Lasallian Center for the Environment will be established to serve as think-tank for the implementation of the identified environmental research themes.

Coastal Management and Integrated Information Management System (IIMS)

The desired capacities along this theme include becoming a functional ICM Learning Center for Luzon with

10 highly proficient ICM trainers. It is hoped to operationalize and sustainably manage IIMS for the province of Batangas and acquire up to date training facilities and capacities. Likewise, it is expected to develop faculty members with advanced degrees in Natural Resource Management and Marine Science. It shall maintain active collaboration with NGOs, LGUs and other sectors in the conduct management and dissemination of CRM-related research and provide easily accessible environmental data available to all stakeholders. It sees itself to spearhead the conduct ICM and IMMS-related training courses.

Biodiversity, Resource Management and Pollution Control

Increasing the number of faculty member with post graduate degrees in Biology and Marine Sciences who are conducting, presenting and publishing relevant research studies is the first and foremost desired capacity on this theme. Streamlining of the biology curriculum into specific sub-fields like Marine Biology and Environmental Biology is deemed necessary. Research findings and recommendation are expected to be well-communicated and translated into policies. It is also hoped to acquire and sustain the operation of the state of the art research lab facilities. In the area of development, it desires to come up with an environmental friendly technology for pollution control.

Mangrove Reforestation and Monitoring Program

As regards this research theme, the desired capacities identified were accomplished baseline research studies on mangroves across the coastal communities of the province of Batangas and conduct of regular community-based monitoring of mangroves. It intends to integrate the mangrove reforestation and monitoring program in the curriculum and to increase the number of mangrove-related research studies completed, presented and published locally and internationally. Such research findings and recommendations are expected to be communicated and translated into policies. Development of advanced technology for mangrove propagation and IEC materials on mangrove conservation are also regarded necessary.

SWOT Analysis on Research Themes

Internal strengths and weaknesses and external opportunities and threats of the institution as regards coastal resource management research vis a vis the research themes were analyzed.

Strengths

Along the theme Integrated Coastal Management and Integrated Information Management System the following strengths were identified: strong partnership with PEMSEA and CI, support from provincial government, presence of information technology experts and functional Information Systems Department with necessary hardware and software requirements in the institution, existence of ICM pool of trainers, strong institutional support.

In terms of Biodiversity Resource Management and Pollution Control Studies, the institutionalized research office with define research thrust and priorities and the existing research laboratory were considered one of the strengths. These are complemented with the technical expertise of faculty members who have completed biological/ environmental research studies by faculty and students. It is worth noting also that the PCR equipment is available in the research laboratory for molecular studies.

The existing Community Involvement Office under the office of the Vice Chancellor for Academics and Research with its adopted communities is considered one of the strengths along the Mangrove Reforestation and Monitoring Program research theme. There is a number of completed baseline mangrove studies conducted faculty and students. The De La Salle Philippines' national projects dubbed as One Million Tress and beyond and the Project Carbon Neutral are also deemed as a strength. The existing GREENER module, which is an environmental recollection module developed by the Science Area and Biology Department, is also an edge of the institution.

Weaknesses

Across the three research themes, the identified internal weaknesses include limited capacity and technical knowledge on information management, GIS applications, data quality assurance and control, and mangrove ecosystem management. The small number of ICM trainers left with limited field exposures of ICM trainers is also regarded as a challenge. In terms of research, teaching workload is seen to possibly hinder research productivity together with the intricacies in institutional research policies unattractive research incentive scheme. The absence of definite departmental research thrust and technical personnel assigned to oversee and supervise the research laboratory is a great problem to deal with by the department and area. H*igh turnover rates of faculty and staff is also a significant consideration.*

Opportunities and Threats

The existing IIMS at PGENRO and the various capacity building programs and funding mechanisms from collaborating institutions are external avenues for the realization of the desired capacities. Support from other NGOs and local government of LIPA and collaboration with other HEIs, schools and other private sectors are also deemed instrumental in the actualization of its goals and vision. This shall also pave the way for forging linkage with technical experts and mentors and attendance to and participation in local and international research presentation and publication. However, the limited funds and the risk of change in administrative priorities are regarded as external threats to the attainment of the said desired capacities.

Research Capacity Gaps

Table 1 summarizes the research capacity gaps that were extracted from the internal weaknesses and external threats identified through the SWOT Analysis done on the theme Integrated Coastal Management and Integrated Information Management System

Table 1. Weaknesses and Research Capacity Gaps on Theme 1

Weaknesses	Research Capacity Gaps
Limited field exposures of ICM trainers	Need for avenues for hands-on ICM training
Limited technical knowledge on resource management	Need for specific skills on resource management
Lack of policy on data sharing and access	Need for IIMS and communication plans
Limited capacity on GIS application	Need for trainings on GIS applications
Limited knowledge on data quality assurance/ control	Need for specific skills on knowledge management

Table 2 presents the research capacity gaps along the theme Biodiversity, Resource Management and Pollution Control.

Table 2. Weaknesses and Research Capacity Gaps on Theme 2

Weakness	Research Capacity Gaps
High turnover rates of faculty and staff	Limited availability of skilful/trained personnel
Teaching work load	Limited time to do research
No departmental research thrust	Need for relevant research framework for the department based on institutional research agenda
Intricacies on institutional research policies	Need for a clear and enabling institutional research policies
No technical personnel assigned in research lab	Need for additional manpower
Limited internal research funding	Need for external funding agencies
Unattractive research incentive scheme	Need for a raise in research incentives
Limited technical knowledge on resource management	Need for specific skills on resource management, pollution control and biodiversity studies
Limited number of research studies completed, presented and published	Need for capacity building on writing proposals, data collection analysis and dissemination to policy makers and scientific writings

The research capacity gaps in line with the Mangrove Reforestation and Monitoring Program theme are reflected on Table 3.

Table 3. Weaknesses and Research Capacity Gaps on Theme 3

Weakness	Research Capacity Gaps
High turnover rates of faculty and staff	Limited availability of skilful/trained personnel
Teaching work load	Limited time to do research
Limited technical knowledge on reforestation and monitoring programs	Need for trainings on mangrove propagation and monitoring
Limited number of research studies completed, presented and published	Need for capacity building on writing proposals, data collection analysis and dissemination to policy makers and scientific writings

Considering the identified research themes, desired capacities, research capacity gaps, an Action Plan was put forward that is further categorized according to priority based on corresponding effort and impact.

References

- Conservation International Philippines. 2013. http://www.conservation.org/global/philippines/about/ pages/about us.aspx (retrieved August 18, 2013)

- McNamara, C. (2011). 'Basics of Action Planning". http://managementhelp.org/ plan_dec/str_ plan/actions. htm (retrieved March 31, 2011)
- PEMSEA.org. 2013. http://www.pemsea.org/ (retrieved August 18, 2013)

ACTION PLAN

Theme 1: Integrated Coastal Management and Integrated Information Management System

Desired Capacity	Research Capacity Gaps	Action Plan	Prioritization	
			Impact	Effort
To become a functional ICM Learning Center for Luzon with 10 highly proficient ICM trainers Operationalized and sustainably managed IIMS for the province of Batangas Up to date training facilities and capacities. Faculty members with advanced de-	Need for avenues for hands-on ICM related works	conduct intensive ICM trainings/workshops for trainers	4	4
		organize field/exposure trips for trainers	2	2
		send representatives to attend pertinent consultations and dialogues	1	3
		conduct training and other capacity building activities among local government units in Luzon	3	1
	Need for specific	initiate the establishment of information network	2	3

<table>
<tr><td rowspan="6">grees in Natural Resource Management and Marine Science.
Active collaboration with NGOs, LGUs and other sectors in the conduct management and dissemination of CRM-related research.
Easily accessible environmental data available to all stakeholders.
Offer ICM and IMMS-related training courses for LGUs.</td><td rowspan="4">skills on information management trainings</td><td>among stakeholders in the province</td><td></td><td></td></tr>
<tr><td>conduct capacity building activities for PG-ENRO, DLSL and coastal communities regarding information management system (e.i. GIS application)</td><td>4</td><td>1</td></tr>
<tr><td>set-up of a physical space to house the IIMS unit</td><td>3</td><td>4</td></tr>
<tr><td>regular updating and maintenance of the IIMS unit</td><td>1</td><td>2</td></tr>
<tr><td rowspan="2">Need for additional manpower and funds</td><td>hire additional personnel</td><td>3</td><td>4</td></tr>
<tr><td>source out funding from partner agencies by sending research proposals</td><td>4</td><td>3</td></tr>
</table>

Theme 2: Biodiversity, Resource Management and Pollution Control Studies

Desired Capacity	Research Capacity Gaps	Action Plan	Prioritization	
			I	E
Increase # of faculty members with post graduate degrees in	Need for specific skills on resource management,	send faculty members to post graduate programs	2	2

<table>
<tr>
<td rowspan="9">Biology and Marine Sciences

Streamlining of the biology curriculum into specific subfields like Marine Biology, Environmental Biology, etc.
. Increased # of faculty members conducting research
. Increased # of research studies completed, presented & published internally and locally
. Research findings and recommendation are well-communicated and translated into policies
. Completed 20 biodiversity assessments of Batangas Province's flora and fauna using Molecular Genetic sequences.
. Acquired and sustained operation of the state of the art research lab facilities
Developed an environmental friendly technology for pollution control.</td>
<td rowspan="3">pollution control and biodiversity studies</td>
<td>organize field/exposure trips for faculty members</td>
<td>1</td>
<td>4</td>
</tr>
<tr>
<td>send faculty members to related trainings and workshops</td>
<td>4</td>
<td>3</td>
</tr>
<tr>
<td>organize write shops/workshops for students and other faculty members and staff (on writing proposals, data collection analysis and dissemination to policy makers and scientific writings)</td>
<td>3</td>
<td>1</td>
</tr>
<tr>
<td rowspan="3">Need for curriculum revision</td>
<td>revisit the existing curriculum</td>
<td>2</td>
<td>4</td>
</tr>
<tr>
<td>benchmark with other HEIs offering same program</td>
<td>4</td>
<td>3</td>
</tr>
<tr>
<td>integrate Marine biology and Environmental biology in the curriculum</td>
<td>3</td>
<td>2</td>
</tr>
<tr>
<td rowspan="3">Need for relevant research framework for the department based on institutional research agenda</td>
<td>conduct a workshop to identify research thrusts of the department</td>
<td>4</td>
<td>4</td>
</tr>
<tr>
<td>align the research thrusts with the identified research themes</td>
<td>3</td>
<td>3</td>
</tr>
<tr>
<td>anchor students theses with the</td>
<td>2</td>
<td>2</td>
</tr>
</table>

		identified research themes		
	Need for a clear and enabling institutional research policies	ask for a dialogue with the ORP	4	3
		draft a proposal regarding revisions on the existing research policies (e.i. raise in research incentives)	3	4
	Need for additional manpower/equipment and external funding agencies	hire additional personnel	2	4
		acquire additional laboratory equipment and reagents	3	3
		source out funding from partner agencies by sending research proposals	4	2

Theme 3: Mangrove Reforestation and Monitoring Program

Desired Capacity	Research Capacity Gaps	Action Plan	Prioritization	
			I	E
. Accomplished baseline research studies on mangroves across the coastal communities of the province of Batangas	Need for specific skills on mangrove reforestation and monitoring	send faculty members to related trainings and workshops	4	4
		organize write shops/workshops for students and	2	3

. Conducted regular community-based monitoring of mangroves . Integrated the mangrove monitoring program in the curriculum . Developed advanced technology for mangrove propagation . Increased # of mangrove-related research studies completed, presented and published locally and internationally. . Developed and disseminated IEC materials on mangrove conservation . Research findings and recommendations are were communicated and translated into policies		other faculty members and staff (on writing proposals, data collection analysis and dissemination to policy makers and scientific writings)		
		conduct workshops on mangrove ecosystem and its importance	3	2
	Need for more community based mangrove monitoring	conduct GREENER for faculty members, staff, students, parents and partner communities	4	4
	Need to integrate mangrove monitoring and reforestation program in the syllabus in environmental science	revisit the existing syllabus	2	2
		deploy school organizations in the community for mangrove planting and monitoring	3	4
		develop IEC materials	4	1
		distribute IEC materials to the students and communities	1	3
	Need for a more scientific technique in	conduct studies regarding mangrove growth rates,	4	3

	mangrove propagation	population structure and dynamics		
		transfer the technology on mangrove propagation to the community	3	4
	Need for venues for research utilization	conduct research forum to communicate the results of the mangrove researches	3	4
		initiate the formation of mangrove alliance among the coastal communities	4	3

Legend:

B. THROUGH ENQUIRING

This technique is done through asking questions. It may be done through an interview, may it be structure formal or informal, through survey questionnaires, attitudinal scales or standardized questionnaires.

Sample 4

Familiarity and Understanding of Chemical Hazard Warning Signs Among Selected College Students: An Action Research

Bernardo C. Lunar, Vivienne Rhea S. Padura, Cristina Franceska T. Dimaculangan

Published in : *Asia Pacific Journal of Multi-disciplinary Research, Volume 2 Number 4, October 2014*

Abstract

Laboratory classes have become crucial parts of teaching science subjects. Most of the laboratories in natural science fields widely use chemicals of different types and hazard levels. Using descriptive- evaluative method, this action research was carried out to assess students' familiarity and comprehension of chemical hazard warning signs. Data were collected from randomly selected 150 student respondents enrolled in Chemistry and Biology Laboratory Classes during the second semester of SY 2012-2013. A structured questionnaire was used for the data collection. The collected data were analyzed using simple quantitative analysis. The results of the study revealed that the majority of the respondents were familiar with hazard signs of laboratory chemicals. After getting information on their level of awareness about potential hazards of laboratory chemicals, the respondents were also requested to match chemicals properties with the corresponding labels or pictograms. The results indicate that familiarity and understanding of hazard warning signs is low among the students. It also surveyed the preferred labelling technique which revealed that majority favored the use of both colors and signs. An action plan was drafted as an output of the study aimed at putting forward corrective measures to address the laboratory related problems identified in the study.

Keywords: Chemical hazards, chemical warning signs, globally harmonized system, laboratory classes

Sample 5.

Assessment of Learning Gains from a Service Learning Activity in Child and Adolescent Development Course

Published in: *IAMURE International Journal of Education Volume 2, March 2012 ISSN 2244-1476 (Print) 2244-1484 (Online)*

Bernardo C. Lunar

Abstract

Exposure trips and service learning as teaching strategies have been proven effective in making students' learning experience more authentic and meaningful. This study looked into the students' self-assessment of their learning gains from the activity dubbed as OrFUN Day (Organized Fun Day)- an exposure trip and service learning activity with the kids in an orphanage. This learning activity was a requirement in Child and Development Course for education students. The 3 Expected Lasallian Graduate Attributes: critical thinkers, excellent communicators, and socially responsible were used as basis for the assessment of perceived learning gains. The student respondents were directed to independently make a thorough case study on their physical development of the kid assigned to them and they were tasked to create a fun-based learning activity that will make them assess the cognitive and socio-emotional development. Students were one in saying that the activity had contributed positively in their learning gains as reflected in their perceived level of attainment of the expected graduate attributes which was high. When the final grades of the students and the attainment of the three graduate attributes were correlated, it was found to have a significant relationship. Students' reflection using the ORID Method of Focused Conversation showed that students regarded the learning experiences as a relevant and purposeful service with the community; as an opportunity to further their academic learning; and as a meaningful civic learning.

Key words: service learning, child development, teacher education, learning gains

Sample 6.

Getting a Grasp of the Experiences of Volunteer Student-Teachers in DREAMS Day Care Center: A Phenomenographic Probe

Bernardo C. Lunar

Abstract

This study probed the lived experiences of the student-teachers as they go through volunteer teaching for pre-school learners at the Dreams Day Care Center. These 2 female volunteer student- teachers are sophomore Generalist Elementary Education students and a BS Education-

Filipino major student. This phenomenography was conducted before the onset of the current pandemic in San Pablo Colleges, Laguna, Philippines SY 2019-2020. The researcher looked into the student teachers' experiences using the ORID Model of Focused Conversation. Based on subjects account of their experiences, it was found out that volunteers are on the same page, they are well aware of their roles and are one in this journey, discovering and learning which took the participants into different realizations during the rendering of service. Delving deeper in the experiences, they develop greater understanding of the teaching profession leading them to grasp the importance of early childhood education. The experience, having impacted their lives, they are propelled to take action positive actions because the experiences led them to appreciate young learners and the teaching profession. Their experiences are linked as the learning outcomes and gains are aligned as they evaluated how the theoretical learnings matched with the actual experience. Learnings are captured, reflections are expressed and realizations are articulated to convey the totality of their experience.

Keywords – volunteer student-teaching, pre-school teaching, phenomenography, San Pablo Colleges

Introduction

Anchored on the San Pablo Colleges' vision of becoming a leading educational institution which nurtures relevant, responsive and value-laden lifelong learning and its mission to uphold the holistic development of learners making them globally competitive through outcomes-based and technology –driven instruction, quality research and proactive community engagement, thereby creating sustainability for all, the College of Education (CED) is committed to the holistic development of the student teachers that are to teach basic education students of the K to 12 Curriculum. Henceforth, its educational program is designed in such a manner that the development in all aspects – spiritual, social, intellectual, emotional, physical and cultural is well-balanced.

The College of Education's share in the community outreach program called DREAMS (Dr. Eufronio Alip Memorial Series), named after the late Dr. Eufronio Alip, one of the founders of San Pablo Colleges is the Day Care Center in the adopted community. Its main objective is to provide early childhood education to the less privileged members of the community in order for them to become productive and self-reliant. The Dreams Day Care Center is located at D.I. Calijan, San Pablo City.

The purpose of this study is to gain an in-depth understanding of volunteer student-teachers' experiences at DREAMS Day Care Center in terms of Objective, Reflective, Interpretive, and Decisional modes This study looked into the experiences of 3 student-teachers from the College of Education of San Pablo Colleges while they were deployed as volunteer teachers in the day care center in the adopted community of the institution. Their experiences were reflected and studied using, the ORID Model of Focused Conversation.

This is study is deemed necessary as this is an initial attempt to describe and understand qualitatively the experiences of volunteer teacher-students vis-à-vis their experiences inter- acting with the parents and the early childhood learners in the day care center. The findings of this study shall serve as valuable inputs for the College of Education and the DREAMS Day Care Center which shall be the basis in ascertaining future directions.

Methods

The research design involved the utilization of qualitative research methods in addressing the research questions. The methodology involved examination of the experiences of the 3 volunteer student-teachers who were deployed for 8 months to teach in the DREAMS Day Care Center from Mondays to Fridays during the Academic Year 2019-2020. The study involved all the three volunteer teachers in the day care center this current Academic Year.

The ORID Model of Focused Conversation was used as data gathering technique. It is a specific facilitation framework that enables a focused conversation with a group of people in order to reach some point of agreement or clarify differences. It was developed by the Institute of Cultural Affairs (ICA) in Canada and involves a facilitator asking people four levels of questioning with each level building on previous levels. It's based on the theory that people need to be cognizant of the actual data and deal with their emotional responses to the topic in order to undertake better analysis and decision-making (Stanfield, 2008). Some notes were taken by the researcher in order to assist in accuracy and transcription, but the note taking was limited to allow the researcher to focus on the participants and their answers to the prompts.

RESULTS AND DISCUSSION

Theme 1: Being on the same page, well aware of their roles.

The participants identified a colorful shade of objective mode towards their volunteering experience. When volunteer respondents were asked about what images or scenes they can recall in DREAMS Day Care center, they all prove to be happy and accomplished. They manifest awareness of their role and the significance of their service. One of the students, participant A, said:

"The images of the children while wearing their smiles on their faces are the scenes that I can always recall during my volunteer teaching. The words from the parents of the children caught my attention because they always express their gratitude towards the volunteer teachers and that makes me really glad. The sounds that I always recall in my mind are my sweet conversations with the children and their genuine laughs. The tactile sensations that I will always recall are the hugs of the kids whenever I enter the classroom and sometimes even when I'm just sitting in the

corner they will come beside me and hug me for no reason, which really make my heart happy".

When participant B was asked of which people, comments, ideas or words caught their attention, she replied:

"The images or scenes that recall in my mind is those smiles and laugh of my students when they are enjoying our lesson and activity. The people that caught my attentions are the parents of the students in the Dreams Day-care that always giving thanks to us teachers for all the loved and efforts that we gave to their children. Why? Because it reminds me / us that we became a part of their lives and we do our job very well.

Particpant C added:

"The sounds that I recall is "Good morning and Good bye" greetings of my students. The tactile sensations that I recall is our morning exercise".

Theme 2: Together all in their journey, discovering and learning.

All participants were asked about their expectations and reflections about the volunteer work before the actual deployment.. The first student, participant A, stated:

"My expectation before volunteering in the day care center was this experience will be exciting and challenging. Exciting because I will have a great time with the kids. Challenging because I will be handling different situations that I know will develop me more not just as a future teacher but also as an individual. My first impression when I met the people in the day care center was they are all very kind and happy. The barangay captain, the councilors, the people in the barangay, and most of all the parents of the children, they are all nice to everyone. Our reaction on the first day in day care center is really a positive one. From the first day until the last day, we are all very happy and thankful of one another. During this experience, I felt excited, challenged, tired, motivated, determined, happy, and grateful"

."

Participant B answered the question as:

"I already expect that it is hard but we can make it until the end. My first impression meeting the people in day care center is that they are very respectful. Even though they know that we are just a 2nd year student. They made us feel like we are already a professional teacher. When I was in the field of teaching I really enjoyed it especially when I saw that my students are learning, it serves as my motivation to study hard and pursue my passion in teaching.".

Everyone else was imagining the same thing as participant B does. When asked about the first impression meeting the pre-school learners in the Center, participant C responded with:

"We have fun teaching there and we will have a great experience there that we can use when we become a full time teacher. They were kind, friendly, and we practiced talking with them and their parents and the kids are so cute and lovely. We are happy because we have new people to meet. It is a great pleasure to meet the children we teach and I love children and it was a great opportunity for us and it is successful."

ON INTERPRETATIVE MODE

Theme 3: Delving deeper in their experiences, developing in-depth understanding.

Along the Interpretative Mode, the participants appreciated the volunteer work more. They also realized the importance of guiding the early learners as future educators. When asked about the most meaningful aspect of being a DREAMS volunteer teacher, participant A answered:

"For me, the most meaningful aspect of volunteering in the day care center is that I/we had the opportunity to teach the kids and be part of their foundation."

Participant B added:

"I had a lot of insights in different aspects from this experience. First, the value of the foundation of education. Next, the importance of good relationship and communication. Another one, having a goal or objective. Lastly, being happy on what you are doing..."

Participant C shared:

"Every day as I walk towards the door of the classroom, I know that it would be another day of tiredness and happiness at the same time. But most of all, it would be another day of opportunity for me to become a part of the lives of those children. So, whenever I enter the classroom I always put in my mind that I need to instill something in the minds of those children. I need to shape one character of these children each day. So, that whenever I went out on that classroom, I can tell myself that I have accomplished something good today"

ON DECISIONAL MODE

Theme 4: Impacting their lives, their passion for teaching intensified.

For the last part of the ORID method of critical reflection, the volunteers were asked on how significant was the experience in their lives as pre-service teachers, and in their lives as students. All participants had their views to share. As for participant A, she answered:

"This experience changed my thinking by making me realize that you will never know how hard a certain thing is until the time that you already experienced it My conclusion from this experience is that if you really want to be a teacher in the future, especially in preschool or elementary, you really need to have the courage, perseverance, and dedication in teaching for shaping and molding your learners...."

Participant B answered the questions as,

"This experience has a significance in my study, work, and life. In terms of my study, it is very significant because I learned how to manage my time and priorities in school. In terms of work, it is very significant as well because it made my eyes open to all the possibilities and challenges that I may face in the future, as an educator. In life, of course it is very significant for me because this experience really developed my perspectives, my skills, my character, and myself as a whole.."

Participant C also also shared:

"In light of this learning I will use it in my journey in becoming a professional teacher in the future. This lesson is something that I will always remember and I will surely bring when I'm already in the field. To be called "Ma'am" is not just enough and I will always put in my mind that I'm

not just a teacher. I am a teacher with a lot of courage, perseverance, and dedication.

Implications

Based on subject's account of their experiences, it was found out that volunteers are on the same page, they are well aware of their roles as they shared almost the same thoughts as regards the objective mode. They are one in the journey, discovering and learning which drove the participants into different realizations during the volunteer work. Delving deeper in the experiences, they developed in-depth understanding of their future roles as educators. The volunteer experiences, having impacted their lives, developed in them more passion for learning and a sincere desire to become a teacher. Their experiences are linked to the program objectives and learning gains are aligned with the program outcomes as they the theoretical learnings are reinforced by the actual experience. Post-pandemic, as soon as everything gets back to normal, efforts shall be made to resurrect the DREAMS Day Care Center and the college shall deploy volunteer student-teachers.

Bibliography

Ash, S. L., & Clayton, P. H. (2009). Generating, deepening, and documenting learning: The power of critical reflection for applied learning. Journal of Applied Learning in Higher Education, 1(1), 25-48.

Beever G. (2017). The ORID Method (Objective, Reflective, Interpretive, Decisional). Retrieved from http://extensionaus.com.au/extension-practice/the-orid-method-objective-reflective-interpretive-and-decisional/

Jacoby, B. (2010). How can I promote deep learning through critical reflection? Magna Publications. Retrieved from http://www.magnapubs.com/mentor-commons/?video=25772a92#.UjnHBazD-70.

Kolb, D. A. 1984, Experiential Learning Experience as the Source of Learning and
(2007). Reflective Practice. A "Critical" Reflection Framework.

C. THROUGH EXAMINING

This is done by looking at records. Sources of data include: archival documents; printed materials like journals and maps; non- print materials like audio and videotapes; artifacts and fieldnotes.

Sample 7. IMPLEMENTERS' EVALUATION OF THE COMMUNITY INVOLVEMENT PROGRAMS OF A PRIVATE SCHOOL IN CALABARZON: AN ACTION RESEARCH

BERNARDO C. LUNAR and JUDITH U. ALCARAZ

Presented: 3rd International Conference on Multidisciplinary Research, February 7-9, 2013, Planta Centro Hotel, Bacolod City

Abstract

De La Salle Lipa, like other higher educational institutions as mandated by the Commission on Higher Education (CHED), has community extension services in the areas of education, livelihood generation, health and nutrition, good governance, technology transfer, environmental awareness and socio-civic and religious matters. This action research study was aimed at assessing the Community Involvement Programs of De La Salle Lipa- College Division. Looking at the participation of the faculty members from each college during the school year 2010- 2011, it was found out that majority of them are rendering more than the required number of hours of either internal or external community involvement. It was noted that all the full-time faculty members of the College of Business, Economics, Accountancy and Management (CBEAM) got the rating 5. As to the evaluation done by the implementers on the general aspect of the community involvement in terms of program description, accountability, understanding and refining, progress towards objectives and program long-term outcomes, the respondents regarded the community involvement programs as highly satisfactory with composite means ranging from 3.33 - 3.69. Assessment of the implementation of the community involvement program using goals-based, process-based and outcomes-based evaluations were also done yielding the following composite mean values, 3. 52, 3.19, and 3.16, respectively. Based on the values, the implementer re relatively lower ratings. As an output, an action plan was put forward to the Community Involvement office to ascertain future directions.

Sample 8. Proposal Title: Assessment of Utilization of the Activity Period: An Action Research

Lunar et al, 2015

Abstract

This action research will assess the utilization of the activity period as perceived by the students, teachers, staff, department/ area chairs and academic deans. Description of the nature of utilization of the activity period will make use of secondary data sourcing from the records of the concerned offices including the deans', department chairs', area chairs, and Students Activities Office. This study will use the descriptive method of research to assess whether the activity period is well utilized or there is a need for it to be modified. The study will employ questionnaires and unstructured interview instruments for data gathering. An action plan/ set of recommendations will be drafted based on the issues/gaps/ problems that will be identified. There has been no assessment of the activity period since its implementation. This assessment and descriptive study of the utilization of the activity period by the different groups of respondents from the college division of De La Salle Lipa are deemed significant to the following: Institution. This will provide baseline data and inputs that will serve as basis for decision making in terms of planning, initiating, implementing and directing the activity period. Colleges. Results of the study will give the college the real picture of utilization as regards activity period. This will allow the respective colleges to assess their utilization of the activity period and make certain future directions. Students. With the end in mind, the beneficiaries will be benefited as utilization of the activity period is assessed, this will ensure that its goals and objectives are met and the gains are maximized.

INTRODUCTION

The establishment and operation of student organizations in all colleges and universities are governed by the rules and regulations established by the Commission on Higher Education (CHED). Students desiring to establish, join and participate in student organizations and activities on DLSL campus may do so as a right, but subject to reasonable regulations promulgated by the institution through the Dean of Students Services (DLSL College Student Handbook, 2011). It is for this reason that the activity period is being implemented, aimed at giving the student organizations time to meet and have their respective activities.

Assessment serves a very essential function in a particular program. It serves as basis for decision making regarding the value and effectiveness of any program. It may take place before, during and after the implementation. Results of this assessment are deemed necessary to ascertain future directions.

The general objective of the project is to assess the utilization of the Activity Period of the college division of De La Salle Lipa. Specifically, the project is aimed to (a) ascertain the nature of utilization of the activity period of the college by the following groups: Students; Teachers; Staff; and Administrators, (b) assess the utilization of the activity period using goals- based assessment; process-based assessment and outcomes- based assessment, and (c) Survey respondents' view on the proposed Activity Day to replace the Activity Period

Review of Literature

Program evaluation can help an organization or an individual to understand, verify or increase the impact of products or services on customers or clients. It can also help improve delivery mechanisms to be more efficient and less costly. It can be useful in verifying that you're doing what you think you're doing. It can facilitate management's thinking about what their program is all about, including its goals, how it meets it goals and how it will know if it has met its goals or not. It can be of use in the production of data or verify results that can be used for public relations and promoting services in the community. Likewise, it is deemed necessary to fully examine and produce valid comparisons between programs to decide which should be retained or be duplicated (McNamara, 2009).

According to Swanson et.al (1996), there are many purposes for undertaking evaluations in any particular situation. One of the reasons for conducting program evaluation is to improve performance. This purpose of evaluation is sometimes called formative since the results are intended to help improve the program during its formative stages. As opposed to summative evaluations when the purpose is to sum up or summarize the accomplishments at a point in time. When evaluations are to improve programs, lessons learned about strengths and limitations of the program are mined from the data so that changes can be made immediately. Sometimes the intent is to discover new approaches and alternatives or to adjust the program to changing situations or client groups. Evaluation also is used to understand multiple reasons for apparent failure or to improve the management or operation of a program.

A school period is a block of time allocated for lessons, classes or other activities in schools (http://www.thefreedictionary...) They typically last between 40 and 60 minutes, with around 3-8 periods per school day. However, especially in higher education, there can be many more. Educators determine the number and length of these periods, and may even regulate how each period will be used. One common example of this practice is to designate at least one compulsory period a day for physical education (Singh, 2010).

The High School Department of the East Tenesee State University implements a 30 minute Activity Period designated specifically for instructional support and enrichment. Components of the program are as follows: Each day, during 30 minutes of the lunch hour, students are assigned to a study room where they have the opportunity to complete school work. Students needing assistance from one of their teachers may see that teacher during this time (http://www.etsu.edu/...) In Marianopolis College, two Activity Periods are universal breaks on Tuesdays and Thursdays from 12:45 – 2:15 pm. This is free time where no classes are scheduled and students have the opportunity to get involved outside of class (http://bemarianopolis....).

A related study by Santos (2011) was conducted to analyze and assess the factors affecting the level of effectiveness of community extension services of college of education in state universities and colleges in Region III.

Based on the findings of the study, the personal profile of those who render the extension nor the community extension service program profile do not affect the level of effectiveness of extension services. Not one from the various factors has significant effects on the level of effectiveness of community extension services in terms of appropriateness and relevance of programs, participation scheme, personnel competence and project effectiveness. An impact assessment of Community Extension Services of St. Joseph Institute of Technology was conducted by Herrera (2010) aimed at examining its impact after rendering three years of extension at Village Lumbocan. Results were based on students and household survey and focus group discussion. Salient findings of this research endeavor confirmed the importance of students to realize their experiential learning that transforms them to become humane individuals who, together with coordinators and volunteers, are committed to be part of the humane extension program at Village Lumbocan.

A related study conducted by Lunar & Alcaraz (2012) assessed the implementation of the community involvement program of De La Salle Lipa college teachers using goals-based, process-based and outcomes- based evaluations were also done yielding the following composite mean values, 3. 52, 3.19, and 3.16, respectively. Based on the values, the implementer respondents considered the implementation of existing community involvement programs as highly satisfactory despite the relatively lower ratings.

An action research study by Parn (2006) involved a classroom of 5thgrade mathematics student engagement levels in the classroom, with a specific interest in how to raise the levels of engagement which students were demonstrating before the study began. Each day, students were given an engagement rubric where they would rate themselves on the previous five criteria. Students enjoyed the opportunity to grade themselves, and their engagement levels significantly improved over the course of the study. It was discovered that giving students specific guidelines and criteria for the expectations, as well as modeling those expectations on the rubric by using pictures, and then having students grade themselves were all key factors to increasing the level of engagement that students demonstrated. As a result of this research, it is planned to continue the use of engagement rubrics not only in the mathematics class, but also in the classes for other subject areas.

METHODS

This study will use the descriptive method of research with the aid of the questionnaire checklist and unstructured interview to assess the utilization of the activity period. The respondents of the study will be the representative samples from the different sectors of DLSL's college division composed including students, teachers, and staff.

The study will use questionnaires and unstructured interview as the instruments for data gathering. The questionnaire will solicit the perceptions of the respondents on the utilization of activity period. Description of the utilization of the activity period by the different sectors will make use of secondary data sourcing from the records concerned offices. The researcher will use 5-point scale parameters and the data will be interpreted using weighted mean.

References

- Cook, T., Eviton, L., Shadish, W. 1991. Foundations of Program Evaluation. Sage Publications, Inc.

- De La Salle Lipa College Student Handbook, 2006-2011

- McNamara, C. 2009. Field Guide to Nonprofit Program Design, Marketing and Evaluation

- Herrera, F. 2010. Impact Assessment of Community Extension Services of Saint Joseph Institute of Technology. JPAIR Multidisciplinary Journal, Volume 4, No. 1

- Parn, L. (2006). An In-Depth Study of Student Engagement. Department of Teaching, Learning, and Teacher Education. University of Nebraska-Lincoln

- Santos, L. 2011. Empowering Communities: The Extension Services of College Education in State Universities and Colleges in Region III.

- Singh, M.K. (2010). The times of India. April 25, 2010. Retrieved on August 24, 2015

- Swanson, R. A., & Holton, E. F., III (2001). Foundations of human resource development. San Francisco: Berrett-Koehler

Bibliography

Argyris, C. (1990). Overcoming organizational defenses: Facilitating organizational learning. Addison-Wesley Longman Publishing Co., Inc.

Asia Pacific Journal of Multi-disciplinary Research (2014) Volume 2 Number 4

Conference Proceedings (2013). 3rd International Conference on Multidisciplinary Research

Global Research Journal on Mathematics and Science Education (2013) Vol. 2 No. 1

Heron, J. (1996). Co-operative inquiry: Research into the human condition. Sage.

IAMURE International Journal of Education (2012) Volume 2

Kemmis, S., & McTaggart, R. (2005). The action research planner (3rd ed.). Deakin University Press.

McTaggart, R. (1997). The participatory inquiry paradigm. The Journal of Applied Behavioral Science, 33(4), 371-390.

Reason, P., & Bradbury, H. (Eds.). (2001). Handbook of action research: Participative inquiry and practice. Sage.

Robson, C. (2002). Real world research: A resource for social scientists and practitioner-researchers (2nd ed.). Blackwell Publishers.

San Pablo Colleges Research Journal (2023) Volume 10

Stringer, E. T. (2007). Action research (3rd ed.). Sage.

LECTURE NOTES ON SCHOOL-BASED MANAGEMENT

A. *Definitions and Importance of School- Based Management*

These definitions highlight the key elements of SBM, including decentralization, empowerment, and active involvement of stakeholders.

"School-Based Management is a decentralized approach to the management of schools, which involves transferring significant decision-making authority and responsibility from central offices to individual schools." (Leithwood & Riehl, 2005)

"School-Based Management is a comprehensive approach to school improvement that empowers teachers, parents, and students to take a leadership role in school decision-making." (Stoll, Louis, & Greenwood, 2003)

"School-Based Management refers to a system of governance in which teachers and other school-based personnel are actively involved in school decision-making and have greater autonomy and responsibility in areas such as budgeting, personnel, and curriculum." (Spillane, Halverson, & Diamond, 2004)

Presented below are the potential benefits of SBM in terms of improved educational outcomes, enhanced accountability, and improved school performance.

"SBM can improve educational outcomes by giving teachers and other school-based personnel more control over their work and creating a culture of shared responsibility for student learning." (Leithwood & Riehl, 2005)

"SBM can enhance school accountability by involving parents and other stakeholders in school decision-making and creating a more transparent and responsive education system." (Stoll, Louis, & Greenwood, 2003)

"SBM can improve school performance by creating a more participatory, collaborative, and empowering work environment for teachers and other school-based personnel." (Spillane, Halverson, & Diamond, 2004)

B. Historical Contexts of School-Based Management

Here is a detailed historical account of school-based management (SBM) provides a more in-depth understanding of the evolution of SBM, from its roots in progressive education to its contemporary role in education reform, with citations for each stage of its development
Progressive Education:

The concept of SBM can be traced back to the progressive education movement of the early 20th century.

Progressive educators, such as John Dewey, advocated for a more democratic and student-centered approach to education, with a focus on teacher autonomy and participatory decision-making (Cremin, 1961).

Post-World War II Era:

In the post-World War II era, there was a growing emphasis on centralization and standardization in education, as governments sought to improve educational outcomes and ensure equal opportunities for all students. This led to a more bureaucratic approach to school administration, with decision-making power concentrated at the district level (Tyack & Cuban, 1995).

Emergence of SBM:

The modern SBM movement emerged in the late 1970s and 1980s, in response to concerns about the inefficiency and lack of accountability of the centralized education system. Proponents of SBM argued that decision-making authority should be transferred from central offices to individual schools, where teachers and other school-based personnel could better respond to the needs of their students (Leithwood & Riehl, 2005).

Implementation of SBM:

SBM gained traction in the 1990s as part of a broader reform movement aimed at improving educational outcomes through greater decentralization, accountability, and collaboration. Many countries, including the United States, Australia, and New Zealand, implemented SBM programs, with varying degrees of success (Stoll, Louis, & Greenwood, 2003).

Contemporary SBM:

Today, SBM remains an important approach to school improvement, with a growing body of research and best practices. While SBM faces ongoing challenges, such as unequal distribution of resources and difficulties in implementing and sustaining effective programs, it continues to be seen as a promising way to empower teachers and improve student outcomes (Spillane, Halverson, & Diamond, 2004).

C. *Common characteristics of school-based management (SBM)*

This list provides an overview of some of the key characteristics of SBM.

1. Decentralization of decision-making:

   SBM involves transferring decision-making authority from central education offices to individual schools, empowering teachers and other school-based personnel to make decisions that best serve the needs of their students.

2. Collaboration and shared responsibility:

SBM is characterized by collaboration among school staff, parents, and other community stakeholders in the decision-making process. This fosters a sense of shared responsibility for student learning and school improvement.

3. Increased accountability:

SBM holds schools and their personnel accountable for student outcomes, promoting greater transparency and efficiency in the education system.

4. Empowerment of teachers:

By giving teachers a greater role in decision-making, SBM empowers them to take ownership of their work and fosters a more positive and supportive school culture.

5. Customization of education:

SBM allows schools to tailor their programs and initiatives to the specific needs of their students and communities, promoting greater flexibility and responsiveness in the education system.

D. *Models of School-Based Management*

Here are some commonly studied models of school-based management

1. Site-based management (SBM):

    This model involves transferring decision-making authority from central education offices to individual schools, empowering teachers and other school-based personnel to make decisions that best serve the needs of their students.

2. Collaborative-based management (CBM):

    This model involves collaboration among school staff, parents, and other community stakeholders in the decision-making process. This fosters a sense of shared responsibility for student learning and school improvement.

3. Empowerment-based management (EBM):

    This model focuses on empowering teachers to take ownership of their work and foster a more positive and supportive school culture. It emphasizes increased decision-making authority for teachers and greater collaboration between teachers and administrators.

4. Centralized-decentralized management (CDM):

   This model involves a balance between centralized decision-making and decentralized decision-making, with schools having the flexibility to make decisions that best serve the needs of their students within the framework of district policies and procedures.

5. Results-based management (RBM):

   This model emphasizes accountability for student outcomes and promotes greater transparency and efficiency in the education system. It involves a focus on student achievement data and the use of that data to inform decision-making and continuous improvement.

E. Stages of Implementation of School-Based Management

The stages of implementation of school-based management (SBM) can vary depending on the specific context and goals. These stages provide a general overview of the process of implementing SBM, though the specific steps and timeline may vary depending on the specific context and goals of the school.

1. Preparation:

   This involves planning and preparing for the implementation of SBM, including defining roles and responsibilities, assessing the school's readiness for SBM, and securing necessary resources and support.

2. Initiation:

   During this stage, the school begins to implement SBM, often starting with pilot projects or small-scale initiatives to build capacity and confidence in the process.

3. Expansion:

   As the school becomes more comfortable with SBM, it can begin to expand the scope and impact of the process, involving more stakeholders and making decisions that have a greater impact on the school.

4. Consolidation:

   During this stage, the school has fully integrated SBM into its day-to-day operations and is committed to continuously improving the process and outcomes.

5. Sustenance:

   This final stage involves ongoing support and evaluation to ensure that SBM continues to be effective and relevant, with regular monitoring of outcomes and ongoing efforts to improve the process.

F. Key Consideration for implementing School-Based Management

Here are some key considerations for implementing SBM.

1. Clearly defined roles and responsibilities

   It is important to clearly define the roles and responsibilities of teachers, administrators, and other school-based personnel in the SBM process. This will ensure that all stakeholders understand their respective responsibilities and are able to effectively collaborate.

2. Strong leadership and collaboration:

   Strong leadership from administrators and teachers, as well as collaboration among all stakeholders, is critical for the effective implementation of SBM.

3. Community involvement:

   SBM is most effective when it involves the active participation of parents, community organizations, and other stakeholders. This promotes a sense of shared responsibility for student learning and school improvement.

4. Adequate resources and support:

   Implementing SBM requires adequate resources and support, including access to data and decision-making tools, professional development opportunities, and adequate staffing.

G. *Best Practices in Implementing School-Based Management*

This list provides an overview of some of the key considerations and best practices for implementing SBM.

1. Use of data and evidence-based decision-making:

   Best practices in SBM involve the use of data and evidence-based decision-making, with a focus on continuous improvement and accountability for student outcomes. (Spillane, Halverson, & Diamond, 2004)

2. Emphasis on teacher empowerment and collaboration:

   SBM is most effective when it emphasizes teacher empowerment and collaboration, fostering a positive and supportive school culture and promoting greater job satisfaction and retention of highly effective teachers.

3. Continuous improvement and adaptation:

   Best practices in SBM involve a focus on continuous improvement and adaptation, as schools respond to changing needs and prioritize the needs of their students and communities.

Bibliography

Cremin, L. A. (1961). The Transformation of the School: Progressivism in American Education, 1876-1957. New York, NY: Vintage Books.

Leithwood, K., & Riehl, C. (2005). What we know about successful school leadership. School Leadership & Management, 25(5), 495-511.
Stoll, L., Louis, K. S., & Greenwood, R. (2003). Teacher leadership: What is it and why is it important? Educational Research, 44(2), 233-250.

Tyack, D., & Cuban, L. (1995). Tinkering Toward Utopia: A Century of Public School Reform. Cambridge, MA: Harvard University Press.

Spillane, J. P., Halverson, R., & Diamond, J. B. (2004). Toward a theory of leadership practice: A distributed perspective. Journal of Curriculum Studies, 36(1), 3-34.

LECTURE NOTES ON ADVANCED EDUCATIONAL PLANNING

A. *Definition and Overview of Educational Planning*

Educational planning refers to the systematic and deliberate process of designing and implementing programs, policies, and initiatives aimed at improving the quality and accessibility of education. It involves the identification of educational needs, the development of goals and objectives, the allocation of resources, and the evaluation of outcomes.

Here are some definitions and overviews of educational planning. These definitions highlight the key elements of educational planning, including the systematic and continuous nature of the process, the consideration of both educational demand and resources, and the goal of improving education quality and accessibility.

"Educational planning refers to the process of formulating strategies, policies, and programs to achieve specific educational goals, and allocating resources to implement them." - UNESCO, World Education Report 2000.

"Educational planning is a dynamic and continuous process of decision making that seeks to balance educational provision with educational demand." - UNESCO Institute for Education, Handbook of Educational Planning.

"Educational planning is a systematic, deliberate, and ongoing process that involves assessing educational needs, setting goals and objectives, allocating resources, and evaluating outcomes." - Adams, D., & Hill, P. (2011). Educational Planning. London: Routledge.

"Educational planning is the systematic and integrated use of resources, including human and material resources, to achieve educational goals and objectives." - United Nations Development Programme, Human Development Report 1990.

B. Importance and Purpose of Advanced Educational Planning

Advanced educational planning is important because it helps to ensure that education systems are responsive to changing needs and challenges, and that resources are allocated in a manner that maximizes their impact. It also helps to ensure that education policies and programs are evidence-based and outcomes-oriented, and that they are designed and implemented in a way that is transparent, accountable, and effective.

The purpose of advanced educational planning is to support the development and improvement of education systems and to ensure that they meet the needs of students, teachers, and society as a whole. This includes identifying and addressing key education challenges, developing strategies to improve the quality and accessibility of education, allocating resources effectively, and continuously monitoring and evaluating the impact of educational policies and programs.

Advanced educational planning also helps to promote equity in education by ensuring that resources are distributed fairly and that all students have access to high-quality education, regardless of their background or socio-economic status. By effectively addressing these issues, advanced educational planning contributes to the long-term development and success of individuals, communities, and societies.

C. Key Concepts and Principles of Educational Planning

The following are key concepts and principles of advanced educational planning. By incorporating these concepts and principles, advanced educational planning helps to ensure that education systems are effective, efficient, and responsive to the needs of students, teachers, and society as a whole.

Evidence-Based Decision Making: The use of research and data to inform decisions about educational policies and programs.

Needs Assessment: The process of identifying the educational needs of students, teachers, and communities and using this information to guide planning decisions.

Goal Setting: The identification of specific and measurable goals and objectives for the education system.

Resource Allocation: The process of determining the most efficient and effective use of resources, including human, financial, and material resources, to achieve educational goals.

Monitoring and Evaluation: The continuous measurement and assessment of the impact of educational policies and programs, with the goal of continuously improving their effectiveness.

Stakeholder Engagement: The involvement of key stakeholders, including students, teachers, parents, communities, and government officials, in the planning process.

Transparency and Accountability: The commitment to open, honest, and accountable decision-making and the use of data and information to inform planning and evaluation.

Equity: The goal of ensuring that all students have access to high-quality education, regardless of their background or socio-economic status.

Flexibility and Adaptability: The ability to respond to changing needs and challenges and to adjust plans and policies accordingly.

Continuous Improvement: The commitment to continuous improvement and the ongoing evaluation and refinement of educational policies and programs.

D. Theories and Models of Educational Planning

There are several theories and models of educational planning, each with a different focus and approach to planning. Each of these theories and models has its strengths and weaknesses, and different approaches may be more suitable for different contexts and situations. Effective educational planning requires a combination of different theories and models, tailored to the specific needs and challenges of the education system. Some of the most commonly used theories and models include:

System's Theory: A holistic approach to educational planning that views the education system as a complex, interrelated set of components that must be understood and managed in a coordinated way.

Needs-Based Planning: A planning model that focuses on identifying the educational needs of students and communities, and using this information to guide decision-making.

Goal-Oriented Planning: A planning model that focuses on setting specific, measurable goals and objectives for the education system, and using these goals to guide decision-making.

Incremental Planning: A planning model that emphasizes the importance of small, incremental improvements to the education system over time, rather than major reforms or overhauls.

Evidence-Based Planning: A planning model that emphasizes the use of research and data to inform decision-making, and the continuous evaluation of policies and programs to ensure their effectiveness.

Network Planning: A planning model that emphasizes the importance of collaboration and coordination among different stakeholders, including schools, communities, and government agencies.

Participatory Planning: A planning model that emphasizes the involvement of key stakeholders, including students, teachers, and communities, in the planning process.

E. Educational Planning Techniques

These are five common techniques used in educational planning:

SWOT analysis - a tool used to identify an organization's strengths, weaknesses, opportunities, and threats.

Needs assessment - a process used to determine the needs and priorities of a community, organization, or individual.

Budgeting and financial planning - involves creating a financial plan to allocate resources effectively and efficiently to achieve goals.

Resource allocation - the process of distributing resources such as time, money, and personnel to achieve goals.

Monitoring and evaluation - a continuous process that assesses the implementation of educational plans and programs and provides feedback for improvement.

F. Challenges and Solutions in Advanced Educational Planning

Challenges in advanced educational planning include:

Limited resources: inadequate funding, personnel, and technology can hinder effective planning and implementation.

Changing needs and demands: the education sector is constantly evolving and changing, making it challenging to keep up with new trends and demands.

Stakeholder involvement: getting all stakeholders (students, teachers, parents, and administrators) on board with the educational plan can be difficult.

Lack of data and research: limited data and research on the effectiveness of certain programs and policies can hinder informed decision-making.

Solutions to these challenges include:

Resource optimization: maximizing resources through effective budgeting, resource allocation, and partnerships with other organizations.

Stakeholder engagement: involving all stakeholders in the planning process to ensure buy-in and support.

Evidence-based decision-making: using data and research to inform educational policies and programs.

Continuous evaluation and improvement: regularly assessing and adjusting educational plans to address changing needs and demands.

Collaboration and partnerships: working with other organizations and institutions to share resources and expertise.

G. Best Practices in Advanced Educational Planning

Here are some successful examples of educational planning:

1. Singapore's Ministry of Education: Singapore's education system is widely recognized as one of the best in the world, and its comprehensive planning system is a key factor in its success. Singapore's Ministry of Education uses data and research to inform its policies and programs, and regularly assesses the needs of students and the education sector to ensure that resources are allocated effectively.

2. Finland's National Board of Education: Finland's educational system is known for its focus on student-centered learning and its innovative approach to educational planning and policy. The National Board of Education works closely with teachers, students, and researchers to develop and implement policies and programs that support student learning and development.

3. New York City Department of Education: The New York City Department of Education has developed a comprehensive system for educational planning and resource allocation that has helped to improve student outcomes and support student success. The department uses data and research to identify areas of need and allocate resources to support the development of effective programs and initiatives.

4. Ontario Ministry of Education: The Ontario Ministry of Education has implemented a system for educational planning that emphasizes stakeholder engagement and collaboration. The ministry works closely with teachers, students, parents, and administrators to identify the needs of the education sector and develop policies and programs that support student learning and development.

References

- "Educational Planning: An Introduction" by Denis R. Lawton

- "The Political Economy of Education: Reforms, Labor Markets and Globalization" edited by Eric A. Hanushek and Ludger Woessmann

- "Planning and Management for a Changing Environment: New Directions for Institutional Research" edited by Jon F. Wergin and Susan Albers Mohrman

- "Educational Planning in Developing Countries" edited by T. Neville Postlethwaite and Rachel Sabates

- "The Handbook of Educational Planning" edited by Richard Simpson and Keith Wragg

- "Strategic Planning for Public and Nonprofit Organizations: A Guide to Strengthening and Sustaining Organizational Achievement" by John M. Bryson

- "The Effective Evaluation of Educational Planning" edited by Ted Garnett and Susan Albers Mohrman

- "Leadership and Management in Education" edited by Tony Bush and David Middlewood

- "School Finance: A Policy Perspective" by Richard F. Elmore and Michael D. Jewett

- "The Future of Education: Policy, Planning and Change in the Asia-Pacific Region" edited by Thomas James and Stephen Dinham.

LECTURE NOTES ON EDUCATIONAL MANAGEMENT AND SUPERVISION

I. Introduction to Educational Management and Supervision

A. Definition and Overview of Educational Management

Educational management is a complex and multifaceted field that requires a wide range of skills and knowledge, including leadership, decision-making, and problem-solving. Effective educational managers must be able to balance the competing demands of different stakeholders, and work towards creating positive learning environments for students.

Educational management can be defined as the process of leading and directing educational organizations (schools, universities, etc.) towards achieving their goals and objectives. It involves a range of activities, including planning, organizing, staffing, directing, and controlling educational programs and resources.

According to the book "Educational Administration: Concepts and Practices" by Fred C. Lunenburg and Allan C. Ornstein, educational management involves the development of educational policies and programs, the allocation of resources, and the creation of an environment that is conducive to student learning. It also requires effective communication and collaboration among stakeholders, including administrators, teachers, students, and parents.

Another definition is provided by "Educational Administration: Theory, Research, and Practice" by Wayne K. Hoy and Cecil G. Miskel, which states that educational management involves creating, maintaining, and improving educational organizations and programs through the application of principles and practices of management. It includes the management of personnel, finances, facilities, and technology, and requires an understanding of the educational context and the needs of stakeholders.

B. Historical Context of Educational Management and Supervision

The concept of educational management and supervision has a long history, dating back to the 19th century with the growth of public education systems. One of the earliest works in this field is "School Management" by Caleb Mills (1839), which provided practical guidance for school supervisors and administrators.

In the early 20th century, the field of educational administration emerged as a distinct discipline, with works such as "The Administration of Public Education" by Paul Klapper (1936) and "The Supervisor and the Su-

pervised" by Harold Rugg (1938). These works emphasized the importance of effective leadership and the role of supervisors in ensuring educational quality.
In the mid-20th century, the field of educational management and supervision became more focused on organizational theory and systems thinking, with works such as "The Principles of Educational Management" by Fred D. Carver and "The Superintendency: Leadership for America's Schools" by Thomas J. Sergiovanni (1984).

In recent decades, the field has shifted towards a more data-driven and evidence-based approach, with a focus on the use of data to improve educational outcomes. Relevant works in this area include "Data-Driven Decision Making in Education" by Douglas B. Reeves (2010) and "Evidence-Based Leadership in Education" by John West-Burnham and Peter Duffy (2013).
Sources:

The historical context of educational management and supervision can be traced back with the development of the public school system and the growth of formal education.

1. "The History of Education: Educational Practice and Progress Considerations" by Ernst Karl Kohlberg (1969)
2. "The Emergence of the Modern Educational System: Structural Change and Social Reproduction, 1840-1920" by Jan De groof (2002)

3. "The Development of American Education: A Historical Overview" by Ronald E. Butchart (2000)
4. "Educational Supervision in Historical Perspective" by J.D. Eggen & D.P. Kauchak (1999)

These works highlight the evolution of educational management and supervision practices and the social, economic, and political factors that influenced their development.

C. Key Goals and Objectives of Educational Management and Supervision

These goals and objectives are interrelated and are essential for ensuring the effectiveness of educational management and supervision. The key goals and objectives of educational management and supervision are as follows:

1. Improving educational outcomes: The primary goal of educational management and supervision is to improve the quality of education and student outcomes. This is achieved through the implementation of effective policies, programs, and practices.
2. Enhancing teacher effectiveness: Another key goal is to support and develop teachers' skills and knowledge, leading to improved student achievement.

3. Ensuring accountability: Educational management and supervision aim to ensure that all stakeholders, including teachers, administrators, and policymakers, are accountable for their actions and decisions.
4. Foster a positive school culture: A positive school culture and a supportive learning environment are critical components of effective education. Educational management and supervision strive to create and maintain these conditions.
5. Resource allocation: Effective educational management and supervision require the effective allocation and use of resources, including funding, personnel, and facilities.
6. Compliance with regulations: Educational management and supervision must ensure that schools and educational institutions comply with applicable laws and regulations.
7. Continuous improvement: Finally, educational management and supervision aim to continuously improve educational outcomes through the use of data, research, and evaluation.

II. Organizational Structures in Education

A. Centralized vs Decentralized Models

Both models have their advantages and disadvantages, and the best organizational structure for an educational institution will depend on its goals, culture, and context.

Centralized:

- In this model, a central authority makes all decisions and controls resources.
- It has a clear chain of command and a hierarchical structure with defined roles and responsibilities.
- Authority flows from the top of the hierarchy to the bottom.
- Decision-making is often more efficient and consistent because there is only one source of power.
- The central authority can enforce policies and procedures, which leads to greater standardization across the organization.
- However, the centralization of power can limit the autonomy of lower-level staff and stifle innovation and creativity.

Examples:

- Bureaucratic model, characterized by hierarchical relationships and formal rules and procedures. (Mintzberg, 1979)

- Top-down management, where decisions are made by a single person or group at the top of the hierarchy. (Robbins et al., 2017)

Decentralized:

- In this model, authority is distributed among multiple individuals or groups.
- There is a flat structure with limited hierarchy, and decision-making is often done through consensus.

- Staff at all levels have a say in decision-making, which leads to greater involvement and ownership among staff.
- Decentralization can promote local innovation and creativity, as staff are given more freedom to experiment and try new ideas.
- However, the lack of a central authority can lead to inconsistency in policies and procedures across the organization, and the complexity of decision-making can be greater.

Examples:

- Flat structure, where decisions are made through consensus and limited hierarchy. (Goldman et al., 2020)

- School-based management, where school staff have significant control over decision-making. (Joyce & Showers, 2002)

B. School Boards and District Management

Both school boards and district management are important components of the educational system, and they work together to provide the best possible education for students. While school boards set policies and provide direction, district management is responsible for implementing those policies and ensuring that the district runs smoothly and efficiently.

School Boards:

- School boards are governing bodies responsible for overseeing the policies and operations of a school district.
- They are typically elected by the public and are accountable to the community.
- School boards set policies and approve budgets, and they hire and evaluate the district superintendent.
- School boards play a critical role in establishing the vision, mission, and goals of the district, and in making decisions that impact student learning.
- They provide a link between the district and the community, allowing for public input and transparency in decision-making.

District Management:

- District management refers to the administrative and operational functions of a school district, including finance, personnel, and facilities management.
- The district superintendent is the chief executive officer of the district and is responsible for implementing the policies set by the school board and managing the day-to-day operations of the district.
- District management also includes other administrators and staff who support the district in its mission to provide high-quality education to students.

C. School Leadership Teams and Organizational Charts

Both school leadership teams and organizational charts are important tools for effective school and district management. School leadership teams provide a collaborative approach to leadership, while organizational charts provide a visual representation of the structure and hierarchy of the organization. Both are critical to promoting clear communication, accountability, and effective decision-making within the educational system.

School Leadership Teams:

School leadership teams are groups of administrators and teachers who work together to lead and manage a school. They are responsible for creating and implementing plans to improve student achievement, and for making decisions that impact the school's operations. School leadership teams typically include the principal, assistant principal(s), and department heads or lead teachers. The team meets regularly to discuss school goals, review data, and make decisions on key issues. The goal of a school leadership team is to provide a collaborative and inclusive approach to school leadership, allowing for the input and perspectives of all stakeholders.

Organizational Charts:

An organizational chart is a visual representation of an organization's structure and hierarchy. It shows the relationships and relative ranks of positions within an organization, and can be used to understand the flow of authority and decision-making. In education, an organizational chart for a school or district would show the relationships between the school board, district management, school leadership teams, teachers, and other staff. Organizational charts can be useful for new staff members to understand the structure of the organization, and for existing staff to see how decisions are made and who is responsible for different functions.

III. Curriculum Development and Instructional Planning

A. Curriculum Design and Implementation

Both curriculum design and implementation are critical to the success of an educational program. Curriculum design provides the blueprint for student learning, while implementation ensures that the curriculum is delivered effectively in the classroom. Effective curriculum design and implementation are essential for promoting student learning and achievement, and for ensuring that students are well-prepared for their future careers and lives.

Curriculum Design:

- Curriculum design refers to the process of creating a plan for the content and structure of a course or educational program.
- It involves identifying learning outcomes, selecting and organizing content, and determining assessment and evaluation methods.

- Curriculum designers consider factors such as student characteristics, state or national standards, and resources available when designing a curriculum.
- Effective curriculum design is based on sound educational principles and research and is informed by data and assessment results.

Curriculum Implementation:

- Curriculum implementation refers to the actual delivery of the curriculum to students in the classroom.
- It involves the teacher's preparation and delivery of instruction, the use of materials and resources, and the assessment and evaluation of student learning.
- Effective implementation requires teachers to understand the curriculum design and the learning outcomes, and to have the skills and knowledge to deliver the curriculum in an engaging and meaningful way.
- Implementation also involves ongoing monitoring and adjustment to ensure that the curriculum is meeting the needs of students and achieving the desired learning outcomes.

B. Instructional Planning and Assessment

Both instructional planning and assessment are critical components of effective teaching and learning. Instructional planning provides the roadmap for student learning, while assessment provides important information about student progress and helps to ensure that the instructional plan is effective. Together, they promote student achievement and provide a solid foundation for effective teaching and learning.

Instructional Planning:

- Instructional planning refers to the process of creating a plan for teaching and learning.
- It involves identifying learning objectives, selecting and organizing content, determining instructional methods, and creating assessment and evaluation strategies.
- Effective instructional planning is based on a clear understanding of the learners and their needs, and is informed by data and assessment results.
- Good instructional planning considers the pacing of the course, the use of technology, and the integration of different subjects or disciplines.

Assessment:

- Assessment refers to the process of evaluating student learning, either formatively (during the learning process) or summatively (at the end of a unit or course).
- It involves the use of a variety of methods, including tests, projects, essays, observations, and self-assessments.
- Assessment provides important information about student learning, and is used to inform instructional planning, adjust teaching methods, and provide feedback to students.

- Effective assessment is aligned with the learning objectives, is valid and reliable, and provides meaningful and useful information to both teachers and students.

C. Understanding Student Learning and Assessment Data

Understanding student learning and assessment data is essential for effective teaching and learning. By using data to inform instruction and assessment, educators can ensure that they are meeting the needs of all students, promoting student achievement, and providing a solid foundation for future success. By analyzing data and using it to make informed decisions, educators can ensure that their efforts are focused on what is most important and that resources are being used effectively to support student learning.

Student Learning:

- Student learning refers to the process by which students acquire knowledge, skills, and understanding through their experiences in school and other settings.
- It involves the active engagement of students in meaningful and relevant learning experiences, and is influenced by a variety of factors, including instruction, motivation, and prior knowledge.
- Effective instruction and assessment practices are important for promoting student learning, and for

ensuring that students are well-prepared for their future careers and lives.

Assessment Data:

- Assessment data refers to information about student learning that is collected through a variety of assessment methods, including tests, projects, essays, observations, and self-assessments.
- Assessment data provides important information about student progress and helps teachers to understand what students know and are able to do.
- Effective use of assessment data involves analysing the results, using the information to inform instructional planning and teaching methods, and providing feedback to students.
- Assessment data can also be used to make decisions about school and district policies, and to inform decisions about resource allocation and professional development.

IV. Human Resource Management in Education

A. Recruitment and Selection of Educators

Recruitment and selection are critical components of effective human resource management in education. By attracting and selecting highly qualified and diverse teachers, schools and districts can ensure that they have the talent and resources necessary to meet the needs of their students and promote student achievement. Moreso, effective recruitment and selection processes help to build strong and supportive school communities, and ensure that teachers are well-prepared to meet the challenges of the classroom.

Recruitment:

- Recruitment refers to the process of attracting and identifying qualified candidates for teaching positions.
- It involves creating and disseminating job advertisements, establishing relationships with universities and other organizations, and engaging in outreach efforts to attract a diverse pool of candidates.
- Effective recruitment efforts consider the specific needs and characteristics of the school or district, and focus on attracting a talented and diverse pool of candidates.

Selection:

- Selection refers to the process of evaluating and choosing the best-qualified candidates for teaching positions.
- It involves reviewing applications, conducting interviews, and using a variety of selection tools and assessments, including reference checks, background checks, and performance assessments.
- Effective selection processes are based on valid and reliable criteria, and consider the fit between the candidate and the school or district, as well as the candidate's qualifications, skills, and experience.

B. Performance Evaluation and Professional Development

Performance evaluation and professional development are critical components of effective human resource management in education. By evaluating performance and providing meaningful and relevant professional development opportunities, schools and districts can ensure that their teachers and other personnel are well-prepared to meet the challenges of the classroom and promote student achievement. Performance evaluation and professional development can help to create a culture of continuous improvement and support the growth and development of the education profession as a whole.

Performance Evaluation:

- Performance evaluation refers to the process of evaluating the effectiveness of teachers and other school-based personnel.
- It involves collecting data on multiple sources, including student achievement, classroom observation, and teacher self-assessment.
- Effective performance evaluations are based on valid and reliable criteria, and provide constructive feedback to teachers to support their growth and development.
- Performance evaluations can also inform personnel decisions, including hiring, promotion, and retention.

Professional Development:

- Professional development refers to opportunities for teachers and other school-based personnel to grow and develop professionally.
- It can take many forms, including workshops, courses, conferences, mentoring, and coaching.
- Effective professional development is aligned with the needs and goals of the individual, the school or district, and the profession, and provides practical and relevant training and support.
- Professional development is an ongoing process that supports the growth and development of teachers and other school-based personnel throughout their careers.

C. Collective Bargaining and Labor Relations

Collective bargaining and labor relations are important components of the education landscape, as they help to establish and maintain the terms and conditions of employment for teachers and other school-based personnel. By engaging in effective collective bargaining and labor relations, school districts and other education employers can ensure that they have the resources and support necessary to attract and retain high-quality teachers, and to promote student achievement. Collective bargaining and labor relations can help to create a supportive and stable working environment for teachers and other school-based personnel, and to promote the growth and development of the education profession as a whole.

Collective Bargaining:

- Collective bargaining refers to the process of negotiating the terms and conditions of employment between an employer (usually a school district or school board) and a union representing teachers and other school-based personnel.
- Collective bargaining agreements typically cover issues such as wages, benefits, working conditions, and the rights and responsibilities of both the employer and the employees.
- Collective bargaining is governed by federal and state laws, and is a key component of the labor relations process in many public sector industries, including education.

Labor Relations:

- Labor relations refer to the relationship between employers and employees, as well as their representatives (e.g. unions), with a focus on the negotiation and resolution of workplace issues.
- Effective labor relations are based on open communication, mutual respect, and a commitment to problem-solving and resolution.
- Labor relations in education are shaped by a variety of factors, including collective bargaining agreements, state and federal laws, and the needs and interests of both the employer and employees.

V. Budgeting and Financial Management in Education

A. Overview of School Budgeting and Financial Management

School budgeting and financial management are critical components of effective educational leadership. By creating and managing budgets and financial resources effectively, schools and districts can ensure that they have the resources necessary to support the needs and goals of their students, and to promote student achievement. Likewise, effective school budgeting and financial management can help to create a culture of accountability, transparency, and responsible stewardship of public resources.

Budgeting:

- School budgeting refers to the process of creating and allocating the financial resources necessary to support the operations and programs of a school or school district.
- It involves forecasting revenues, estimating expenditures, and making decisions about how to allocate resources to support the priorities of the school or district.
- Effective school budgeting is based on accurate and reliable data, and is driven by a clear understanding of the needs and goals of the school or district.

Financial Management:

- Financial management in education refers to the responsible and effective use of financial resources to support the operations and programs of a school or school district.
- It involves the development and implementation of sound financial practices, policies, and systems to ensure the efficient and effective use of financial resources.
- Effective financial management in education requires a strong understanding of the financial landscape of the school or district, including revenue sources, expenditures, and budget constraints.

B. Allocating Resources and Making Decisions

Resource allocation and decision making are critical components of effective educational leadership. By making informed and strategic decisions about the use of resources, school and district leaders can ensure that they are supporting the needs and goals of their students and promoting student achievement. Furthermore, effective resource allocation and decision making can help to create a culture of continuous improvement and support the growth and development of the education profession.

Resource Allocation:

- Resource allocation refers to the process of deciding how to distribute resources (e.g. financial, human, physical, etc.) to achieve specific goals and objectives.
- In education, resource allocation involves making decisions about how to use available resources to support the operations and programs of a school or school district.
- Effective resource allocation requires accurate data, a clear understanding of the needs and goals of the school or district, and a focus on achieving the greatest possible impact with available resources.

Decision Making:

- Decision making refers to the process of selecting a course of action from among multiple options.
- In education, decision making involves making choices about the allocation of resources, the design and implementation of programs and initiatives, and the direction and focus of the school or district.
- Effective decision making requires accurate information, a clear understanding of the context and constraints, and a focus on achieving the greatest possible impact.

C. Working with External Funds and Grants

Working with external funds and grants is an important component of effective educational management and supervision. By leveraging these resources, schools and districts can access additional financial support to support their operations and programs, and to promote student achievement. Moreover, working with external funds and grants can help to build partnerships and relationships with key stakeholders, and can provide valuable opportunities for professional growth and development.

External Funds:

External funds refer to resources that are available to a school or school district from sources outside of the organization. These funds may come from private foundations, corporations, government agencies, or other organizations, and may be used to support specific programs, initiatives, or activities. Effective use of external funds requires a strong understanding of the available resources and the process for accessing and utilizing these funds.

Grants:

Grants are a specific type of external funding that are awarded by a funder (e.g. foundation, government agency, corporation, etc.) to support specific programs, initiatives, or activities. Grant funding may be used for a wide range of purposes, including program implementation, professional development, research, and more. Effective use of grants requires a strong understanding of the grant application process, the goals and priorities of the funder, and the needs and goals of the school or district.

VI. School Safety and Emergency Management

A. Requirements and Best Practices

School safety and emergency management requires a comprehensive and proactive approach, including:

1. Developing emergency plans and drills: The school should have written plans for various emergency scenarios, such as natural disasters, fires, active shooter incidents, and evacuation procedures. Regular drills help ensure students and staff know how to respond.
2. Providing staff training: Regular training for all school staff on emergency procedures and response is essential.
3. Physical security measures: This includes measures like secure entry points, cameras, and visitor management systems to monitor who enters the building.
4. Threat assessments: The school should regularly assess and address potential safety threats to identify potential risks and prevent them.
5. Mental health support: Providing mental health support and resources to students and staff can help

identify and address potential threats before they become emergencies.

6. Collaboration with local law enforcement and first responders: Schools should maintain strong relationships with local emergency responders to ensure quick response in the event of an emergency.
7. Emergency communication systems: An effective emergency communication system should be in place to quickly notify and provide information to students, staff, and parents during an emergency.
8. Review and updating plans: Regularly reviewing and updating emergency plans is crucial to ensure they remain effective and relevant.

B. Developing and Implementing Emergency Response Plans

Here are the suggested steps to follow when developing and implementing emergency response in schools:

1. Assess risks: Identify potential emergency scenarios and evaluate their likelihood and impact.
2. Define roles & responsibilities: Assign clear roles and responsibilities for responding to emergencies.
3. Establish protocols: Develop detailed procedures for responding to specific emergency situations.
4. Train personnel: Provide training for all personnel on emergency response procedures and drills.

5. Test & refine: Regularly test emergency response plans through drills and simulations, and revise plans as needed.
6. Ensure communication: Establish clear lines of communication among responding parties and with external agencies.
7. Obtain necessary resources: Ensure adequate resources, such as equipment and supplies, are available for emergency response.
8. Review & update: Regularly review and update emergency response plans to keep them current and effective.

C. Training and Preparing School Personnel

Here are the suggested trainings for teachers and school personnel:

1. Awareness training: Provide basic training for all personnel on emergency response procedures and policies.
2. Evacuation drills: Conduct regular evacuation drills to familiarize personnel with emergency exits and procedures.
3. Active shooter training: Provide training on how to respond to active shooter incidents.
4. First aid & CPR: Offer training in first aid and CPR to designated personnel.

5. Threat assessment: Establish a threat assessment process to identify and address potential threats to school safety.
6. Emergency communication: Establish clear lines of communication during emergencies and ensure personnel know how to use emergency communication systems.
7. Crisis management: Develop a crisis management plan and train designated personnel on how to respond to critical incidents.
8. Regular drills & exercises: Regularly conduct emergency response drills and exercises to test preparedness and refine response plans.
9. Collaboration with first responders: Foster strong relationships and establish clear protocols for collaboration with local first responders.

VII. Community Relations and Outreach

A. Engaging Parents and Community Stakeholders

Engaging parents and community stakeholders is crucial for building strong community relations and effective outreach efforts. Here are a few best practices for engaging parents and community stakeholders:

1. Regular communication: Regular and transparent communication with parents and community members can help build trust and support for the school.

This can be achieved through newsletters, community meetings, and other forms of outreach.

2. Parent and community involvement: Encouraging and facilitating parent and community involvement in school events, volunteer opportunities, and decision-making processes can help build stronger relationships.
3. Listening and responding to feedback: Actively listening to the concerns and feedback of parents and community members and responding appropriately can help address issues and build trust.
4. Collaborating with community organizations: Collaborating with local businesses, non-profits, and other community organizations can help build relationships and support for the school.
5. Celebrating diversity and inclusivity: A school that celebrates and values the diversity of its students, families, and community members can help build a more supportive and inclusive environment.
6. Providing opportunities for education and involvement: Providing opportunities for parents and community members to become more informed and involved in the school can help build a stronger relationship and understanding.

B. Building Positive Relationships with Local Businesses

Building positive relationships with local businesses can help a school enhance its community outreach efforts and provide additional support for students and staff. Here are a few best practices for building positive relationships with local businesses:

1. Networking and outreach: Building relationships with local businesses can start with networking and outreach efforts, such as visiting local businesses and inviting business representatives to school events.
2. Partnering for joint projects: Schools can partner with local businesses on joint projects or initiatives that benefit both the school and the local community.
3. Encouraging business involvement: Encouraging local businesses to get involved in the school community through volunteer work, donating resources, or sponsoring events can help build positive relationships.
4. Utilizing business expertise: Schools can utilize the expertise of local businesses to provide students with real-world learning experiences, such as job shadowing or internships.
5. Acknowledging business support: Acknowledging and showing appreciation for the support provided by local businesses can help strengthen relationships and encourage continued support.
6. Collaborating on community events: Collaborating with local businesses on community events and initiatives can help bring the school and local business community together.

C. Developing and Implementing Community Outreach Programs

Developing and implementing effective community outreach programs can help build strong relationships between the school and the surrounding community. Here are a few steps for developing and implementing community outreach programs:

1. Identify needs and goals: Identify the needs and goals of the school and the surrounding community, and assess how a community outreach program can address these needs and achieve these goals.
2. Engage stakeholders: Engage key stakeholders, such as school administrators, teachers, parents, community leaders, and local businesses, in the development and planning of the outreach program.
3. Develop a plan: Develop a detailed plan for the outreach program, including goals, objectives, target audiences, timeline, budget, and methods for measuring success.
4. Secure resources: Secure the resources necessary to implement the outreach program, such as funding, volunteers, and materials.
5. Implement the program: Implement the outreach program, and be flexible and adaptable as needed to ensure its success.
6. Evaluate and adjust: Regularly evaluate the outreach program to assess its impact and identify areas for improvement, and make necessary adjustments to ensure its continued success.

VIII. Future Trends in Education Management and Supervision

A. Emerging Issues and Challenges

Emerging issues and challenges in educational management and supervision can impact the effectiveness of schools and the success of students. Here are a few of these emerging issues and challenges:

1. Technology integration: The increasing use of technology in education requires effective management and supervision to ensure that technology is being used effectively and securely.
2. Diversity and inclusivity: Ensuring that all students feel valued and supported, regardless of their background, is becoming increasingly important and requires effective management and supervision.
3. Mental health and well-being: The well-being of students, including their mental health, is becoming a growing concern, and effective management and supervision are necessary to address these issues.
4. Remote and hybrid learning: The rise of remote and hybrid learning due to the COVID-19 pandemic has presented new challenges for educational management and supervision, including ensuring equity and access to technology.
5. Budget constraints: Tight budgets and limited resources are becoming increasingly common and can impact the ability of schools to provide necessary support and resources for students and staff.

6. Teacher shortages: A shortage of qualified teachers in certain subjects or areas is becoming a growing challenge, requiring effective management and supervision to ensure that schools are staffed with qualified teachers.

References

- Carver, F. D. (1949). The Principles of Educational Management.
- Goldman, S. L., Schmitt, N., & Bartel, C. A. (2020). Psychological and organizational behavior. Routledge.
- Hoy, W. K., & Miskel, C. G. (2008). Educational administration: theory, research, and practice (9th ed.). McGraw-Hill Education.
- Joyce, B., & Showers, B. (2002). Student achievement through staff development (3rd ed.). ASCD.
- Klapper, P. (1936). The Administration of Public Education
- Lunenburg, F. C., & Ornstein, A. C. (2010). Educational administration: concepts and practices (8th ed.). Wadsworth/Cengage Learning.
- Mills, C. (1839). School Management.

- Mintzberg, H. (1979). The Structuring of Organizations. Englewood Cliffs, NJ: Prentice Hall.
- Reeves, D. B. (2010). Data-Driven Decision Making in Education.
- Robbins, S. P., Judge, T. A., & Sanghi, S. (2017). Organizational behavior. Pearson.
- Rugg, H. (1938). The Supervisor and the Supervised.
- Sergiovanni, T. J. (1984). The Superintendency: Leadership for America's Schools.
- West-Burnham, J., & Duffy, P. (2013). Evidence-Based Leadership in Education.

LECTURE NOTES ON EFFECTIVE APPROACHES & STRATEGIES FOR TEACHING STEM

1. *Hands-on and project-based learning:*

Students are encouraged to engage in hands-on activities and projects that allow them to apply their knowledge of STEM concepts in real-world scenarios. Hands-on and project-based learning (PBL) are teaching strategies that prioritize student engagement and active participation in learning.

Examples of hands-on learning activities in STEM education include:

- Building models or prototypes to demonstrate understanding of scientific concepts
- Conducting experiments or simulations to test hypotheses
- Manipulating physical materials to explore mathematical concepts.

Examples of project-based learning in STEM education include:

- Designing and building a bridge or tower to demonstrate an understanding of engineering principles

- Developing a business plan to explore economic concepts
- Creating a computer program to solve a real-world problem

Both hands-on and project-based learning provide students with opportunities to apply what they have learned, think critically, and work collaboratively. Additionally, PBL often requires students to work on extended projects over several weeks or months, which allows them to dive deeper into a topic and develop a more comprehensive understanding.

2. Inquiry-based learning:

This is employed by encouraging students to ask questions, make observations, and engage in problem-solving activities to drive their own learning. Inquiry-based learning is a teaching strategy that emphasizes student-led investigation and discovery. In an inquiry-based classroom, students are encouraged to ask questions, make observations, and engage in problem-solving activities to drive their own learning.

Examples of inquiry-based learning activities in STEM education include:

- Asking students to formulate a question about a scientific phenomenon and design an experiment to test it

- Encouraging students to explore and make connections between different mathematical concepts
- Allowing students to conduct research on a topic of their choice, and then presenting their findings to the class

Inquiry-based learning allows students to take an active role in their own education, and encourages them to think critically and creatively. Additionally, it can help students develop important research skills, such as forming hypotheses, collecting data, and presenting findings. By taking a student-centered approach to learning, inquiry-based instruction can also increase student engagement and motivation in STEM subjects.

3. Collaborative learning:

This is done by creating opportunities for students to work together in groups to solve problems and share ideas. Collaborative learning is a teaching strategy that involves students working together in groups to solve problems and share ideas. This approach can foster a supportive learning environment and help students develop important 21st century skills, such as communication, teamwork, and problem-solving.

Examples of collaborative learning activities in STEM education include:

- Having students work in small groups to design and build a project, such as a bridge or a robot
- Assigning students to work together on a problem-solving task, such as finding the most efficient way to sort a pile of items
- Encouraging students to share their findings and ideas during class discussions and group presentations

Collaborative learning can also help students to better understand STEM concepts by hearing different perspectives and approaches. It can also provide opportunities for students to practice communication skills and develop teamwork, which are valuable in both academic and professional settings.

4. Technology integration:

This strategy involves the use of technology such as computers, interactive simulations, and virtual labs to enhance students' understanding of STEM concepts.

Examples of technology integration in STEM education include:

- Using computer simulations to model complex scientific phenomena, such as the behaviour of atoms or the spread of a disease

- Providing students with access to online resources and educational software to support learning and exploration
- Utilizing virtual labs to conduct experiments and gather data, without the need for physical equipment
- Incorporating interactive simulations and visualizations to enhance understanding of mathematical and scientific concepts

Technology integration can provide students with new and engaging ways to explore STEM subjects, and can help to increase their understanding of abstract concepts. Additionally, technology can provide students with opportunities to develop important 21st century skills, such as digital literacy and problem-solving. By incorporating technology into STEM instruction, teachers can also create a more dynamic and interactive learning environment.

5. Real-world connections:

This is done by making connections between STEM concepts and their real-world applications to increase students' relevance and engagement. Making real-world connections in STEM education refers to the practice of connecting abstract concepts and theories to their practical applications in the real world. This approach can increase student engagement and relevance by highlighting the practical significance of STEM subjects.

Examples of making real-world connections in STEM education include:

- Discussing current events or real-world problems related to STEM subjects, such as climate change or natural disasters
- Connecting mathematical concepts to real-world situations, such as budgeting and financial planning
- Highlighting the practical applications of scientific concepts, such as the use of renewable energy sources
- Inviting professionals from STEM fields to speak to students about their work and the impact it has on society

Making real-world connections can also help students to see the relevance and importance of STEM subjects, and can motivate them to engage more deeply in their studies. By highlighting the practical applications of STEM concepts, teachers can help students understand why they are learning what they are learning, and how they can use their knowledge to make a positive impact in the world.

6. Assessment for learning:

It is a teaching strategy that uses assessment as a tool to support and enhance student learning, rather than simply as a means of evaluating performance. In STEM instruction, assessment for learning can involve a variety of activities and techniques, including formative assessments, self-reflection, and peer assessment.

Examples of assessment for learning in STEM education include:

- Using formative assessments, such as quizzes or exit tickets, to check for understanding and provide feedback to students
- Encouraging students to reflect on their own learning and progress, and to set goals for improvement
- Providing opportunities for students to receive feedback from their peers, such as through peer review or group presentations
- Incorporating performance tasks, such as creating a model or designing a solution to a real-world problem, that allow students to demonstrate their understanding in a hands-on and authentic way

Assessment for learning can help students to understand their strengths and weaknesses, set goals for improvement, and develop a growth mindset. It can also provide teachers with valuable information about student understanding and progress, which can inform instructional decision-making and help to ensure that all students are making progress towards their learning goals. Additionally, by using a variety of assessment strategies and techniques, teachers can provide students with a more comprehensive and authentic picture of their learning.

7. Garden-Based Learning:

School and community gardens can be used for academic enrichment, where students can learn about nutrition, food security, and ecological sustainability. Garden-based learning is a teaching strategy that involves incorporating hands-on, outdoor learning experiences in a garden or other natural setting into STEM instruction. This approach can provide students with opportunities to engage with the natural world, explore scientific concepts in a real-world context, and develop important 21st century skills such as critical thinking, problem-solving, and collaboration.

Examples of garden-based learning in STEM education include:

- Conducting plant and soil science experiments, such as monitoring plant growth or testing soil pH
- Using a garden as a living laboratory to explore topics such as ecosystems, photosynthesis, and food webs
- Incorporating mathematical concepts into garden design and planning, such as calculating area and volume, or measuring distances and angles
- Engaging in interdisciplinary projects that integrate STEM subjects with other areas of study, such as language arts or social studies

Garden-based learning can also provide students with a deeper appreciation for nature and the environment, and can help to cultivate a lifelong interest in STEM subjects. Additionally, this approach can help to engage students who may have difficulty with more traditional classroom-based instruction, and can provide opportunities for hands-on, experiential learning.

8. Service Learning:

An educational approach where a student learns theories in the classroom and at the same time volunteers with an agency (usually a non-profit or social service group) and engages in reflection activities to deepen their understanding of what is being taught. Service learning is a teaching strategy that involves incorporating community service projects into STEM instruction. This approach can provide students with opportunities to apply their STEM knowledge and skills to real-world problems, and to engage in service-based activities that make a positive impact on their communities.

Examples of service learning in STEM education include:

- Partnering with local organizations or businesses to address community needs, such as conducting energy audits or creating sustainable transportation solutions

- Engaging in STEM-related service projects, such as designing and building technology solutions for non-profit organizations or community groups
- Incorporating technology and engineering principles into service projects, such as creating websites or developing software to support community organizations
- Providing students with opportunities to conduct research projects in support of community initiatives, such as studying the impacts of environmental degradation or developing solutions to local environmental challenges

Service learning can provide students with a deeper understanding of the ways in which STEM subjects can be applied to real-world problems, and can help to foster a sense of civic responsibility and social awareness. Additionally, this approach can provide students with opportunities to develop important 21st century skills, such as critical thinking, problem-solving, and collaboration.

References

1. Barab, S. A., & Duffy, T. M. (2000). From practice fields to communities of practice. The Design of Learning Environments, 1(1), 9-30.

2. Bowers, J., & Flinders, D. J. (2011). Design-based research and educational technology. Educational Technology Research and Development, 59(1), 5-14.

3. Hand, B., Prain, V., & Tytler, R. (2012). Drawing on science: The role of drawing in learning and teaching science. Science Education, 96(1), 28-50.
4. Herrenkohl, L. R., Palincsar, A. S., DeWater, L. S., & Koper, S. S. (2002). Designing environments for constructive learning. Educational Psychologist, 37(3), 165-174.

5. Linn, M. C., & Hsi, S. (2000). Computers, teachers, peers: Science learning partners. Review of Educational Research, 70(2), 141-178

6. Michael, J. (2007). The nature of mathematics. The Mathematics Educator, 17(1), 1-5.

7. Mestre, J. P. (2012). Learning and Transfer: A Scientific and Technological Approach. Springer Science & Business Media.

ABOUT THE AUTHOR

DR. BERNARDO C. LUNAR is the Dean and Director of the Graduate School and concurrently the Director the Office of Research, Evaluation and Publication of San Pablo Colleges. He holds a Doctor of Philosophy Major in Educational Management and Master of Education in Science Education. He has undergraduate degrees in Bachelor of Science in Physical Therapy and Bachelor of Science in Education major in Science. His research interests include Science Education, environmental conservation and plant ecology. He has authored and co-authored Science books and has published research articles in various reputable local, national, regional and international ISI journals. He has been given various awards by local and international organizations like Luminary Award in Research 2021, Outstanding World Research Leader 2013, Outstanding Filipino Research Leader 2013, and Outstanding

Asian Researcher 2012 for his contributions in the field of educational and environmental research.

www.ingramcontent.com/pod-product-compliance
Lightning Source LLC
LaVergne TN
LVHW052030170826
845678LV00018B/2260

* 9 7 8 6 2 1 4 7 0 4 7 2 9 *